CW01024272

Public Policy Beyond Trad

A Maqāṣid Approach

PUBLIC POLICY BEYOND TRADITIONAL JURISPRUDENCE

•

A Maqāṣid Approach

BASMA I. ABDELGAFAR

IIIT
LONDON · WASHINGTON

IIIT, P.O. BOX 669, HERNDON, VA 20172, USA • www.iiit.org
P.O. BOX 126, RICHMOND, SURREY TW9 2UD, UK • www.iiituk.com

ISBN 978-1–56564–375–8 *limp*
ISBN 978-1–56564–376–5 *cased*

Typesetting and cover design by Shiraz Khan
Printed in the USA

TO MY MOTHER

CONTENTS

FOREWORD

Reality demonstrates that the wide fiscal and regulatory powers of Muslim governments today do not seem to have redressed the acute social and economic problems plaguing most Muslim societies. A fundamental aspect of good governance, broadly identified as equitable management of affairs in favor of citizenry, is public policy and implementation of democracy in the decision-making process. What is the role of *maqāṣid al-sharīʿah* in this?

Government of any form can only operate on the basis of a set of assumptions. *Maqāṣid al-sharīʿah* plays an important role in that it acts as a guide and sets the framework within which assumptions, goals and actions can be defined, to improve government functioning, remove corruption, and deliver the most equitable service to citizens. The marriage of *maqāṣid al-sharīʿah* to public policy thus establishes boundaries, emphasizes responsibilities, sets priorities, and ultimately brings a Divine perspective into the conversation of how a government defines policies. *Shūrā* for instance being an important postulate of this, to give democratic voice to ordinary people whose very quality of life is impacted on a day-to-day basis by decisions they have no say in.

The chapters in this book examine the contribution of *maqāṣid* studies to public policy in Islam. Each chapter deals with a specific theme that together offer an introduction to this area of study. There is no doubt that the ideas presented are in need of further development. Policy and governance are very complex issues. A discipline cannot be born without the existence of a critical mass of dedicated researchers capable and willing to produce seminal works to form its foundations. The author's travels throughout the world have convinced her that there is a strong and growing interest in the potential of *maqāṣid al-sharīʿah* to support this endeavor.

Foreword

Where dates are cited according to the Islamic calendar (hijrah) they are labelled AH. Otherwise they follow the Gregorian calendar and are labelled CE where necessary. Arabic words are italicised except for those which have entered common usage. Diacritical marks have been added only to those Arabic names not considered modern.

Since its establishment in 1981, the IIIT has served as a major center to facilitate serious scholarly efforts. Towards this end it has, over the decades, conducted numerous programs of research, seminars and conferences, as well as publishing scholarly works specialising in the social sciences and areas of theology, which to date number more than six hundred titles in English and Arabic, many of which have been translated into other major languages.

We would like to thank the author, as well as the editorial and production team at the IIIT London Office, and all those who were directly or indirectly involved in the completion of this book. May God reward them for all their efforts.

IIIT PUBLICATION AND
TRANSLATION DEPARTMENT

June, 2018

PREFACE

This book is a collection of seven chapters that examine the contribution of *maqāṣid* scholarship to critical topics in public policy in Islam. Although there is a common thread linking the chapters, each presents an independent argument and as such each chapter can be read independently of the others. The main motivations for this effort were two-fold: first, I sought to demonstrate that the *maqāṣid** approach is indispensable to the theory and practice of public policy in Islam. That said, it is clear that the discipline is in an embryonic stage, still requiring critical contributions in every relevant subject. Second, I wished to write from a policy, not political science, perspective. The latter forms the vast majority of productions by Islamic scholars who are not directly involved in Islamic jurisprudence thereby leaving a void in proper policy studies.

Public policy in Islam is a qualitatively different enterprise for scholars, students and practitioners from both jurisprudence (fiqh) and Shariᶜah-oriented politics (*siyāsah sharᶜīyah*). The absence of preference for a specific political system in the Qur'an, for instance, is recognized as an appeal to focus on what we do in and through institutions as opposed to their actual design or the religious identities and motivations of leadership. The obligation to practice *shūrā*, a form of collective decision-making, imposes criteria on the nature of institutions that produce public policy which conforms with Islamic procedures and substance but does not dictate their final form. The participatory nature of *shūrā* highlights the role of persuasion in

* These are slight variations in meaning of the word *maqāṣid*, the usage of which depends on the context of the term in Arabic or the explicit definition articulated by different scholars. Generally, *maqāṣid* encompasses all these meanings.

Islamic governance processes. Public policy must necessarily be subject to the engagement of experts and interested stakeholders. It must also seek to carry the general public that collectively bears the consequences of policy making. This approach does not tolerate the 'unrestricted interests' (*al-maṣāliḥ al-mursalah*) approach of Shariʿah-oriented politics or the command style approach of jurisprudence where issuing edicts is habitual.

In light of this, public policy in Islam is neither pure art nor pure science but rather includes elements of both. Its art and craft lies in the ability to identify, develop and present alternatives in ways that persuade multiple stakeholders as to the preference of a specific course of action. It is a science to the extent that it is based on the body of knowledge available in the primary sources of the Qur'an and Sunnah. Although such knowledge is not presented in a systematic way, the elements of building robust systems are available in a form that allows succeeding generations to draw upon those elements that will allow each to deal effectively with the challenges they face. This underscores the principle of relevance in Islamic policy studies. The integrated and purposeful reading of the Revealed and unrevealed word is intended to provide individuals and larger social units with the knowledge that they can seize upon and use to understand and address prevailing phenomena.

The scholarship concerned with *maqāṣid al-sharīʿah* or the objectives of Divine law present an indispensable contribution for this purpose. *Maqāṣid* scholarship has distinguished itself from other Islamic approaches, and in particular traditional jurisprudence, through an emphasis on purposefulness, value premises and priorities, as well as openness to multi-disciplinarity and multi-methods. The approach's revival by a number of renowned contemporary scholars represents a six-fold attempt to (1) distance the Shariʿah from the whims of jurists whose legal edicts neglect the higher objectives of Divine law including mercy, equity, wisdom and welfare as well as from the actions of political actors who draw upon the latter to further oppression and corruption; (2) rebut contemporary and largely secular but also Muslim assertions that Islam is an archaic, unjust and violent system of belief; (3) search for explanations as to why, on a general level, the affairs of Muslim communities do not reflect the Divine injunction of human dignity; (4) provide an alternative to the narrow juristic lens that has dominated traditional discourse in order to revive Islam both in the Muslim world and universally; (5) present scholars in other disciplines with the key to incorporate Islamic studies in their respective domains and the lay believer to revert to the use of his or her inherent sense of morality and values; and (6) propose criteria for re-unifying the ummah.

The scope of this enterprise and the desire to reach a broad spectrum of people impacts the nature of the language that can be used to articulate ideas. Although a notable hallmark of the policy sciences is the absence of a widely used professional language, this is even more pronounced in a work that seeks to integrate *maqāṣid* scholarship with policy, and even more, one that acknowledges and respects the dynamics of belief in this enterprise. The professionalization of fiqh through the rules of *uṣūl al-fiqh* has been accompanied by the development of a professional language that is not accessible to the vast majority of non-experts. This is also true of the field of *siyāsah sharʿīyah*. The world of religious-legal scholarship is not only mostly closed to those from outside the discipline, it does not admit the inclusion of new terminology without much consternation. When the top scholars talk, they are talking to each other, communicating and convincing each other of the need for marginal changes. Generally, their concern for guarding a vast legal inheritance far outweighs a concern with the intricacies of today's public interests or critical phenomena. This is not acceptable in policy studies and does not reflect its theory and practice in the Qur'an and Sunnah. Therefore, my overriding concern in producing this work has been accessibility.

This work has also demanded an intense reflection on available English translations of the Qur'an. Any work of translation is also necessarily one of interpretation. Although there are several reputable translations of the Qur'an in English, many do not capture the essence of certain critical Arabic words and their meanings. Given the importance of accurate understanding and by association translation of the Qur'an for a project of this nature, I have translated the Qur'anic verses myself. Professor Jasser Auda graciously reviewed all translations for confirmation of accuracy.[1] All Qur'anic references are included within brackets in the body of the text unless there is reference to three or more verses.

I hope, despite its simplicity, that it is useful for individuals and groups interested in what Islam has to say on a number of key public issues. The chapters in this book focus on macro rather than micro concerns. Consideration of specific policy areas will be the subject of future studies. These chapters offer a series of connected ideas about what the application of a *maqāṣid* approach to public policy and governance looks like so that we can not only make and critique public policy but more importantly so that we can assess the claims of others. Over fourteen centuries have passed since Prophet Muhammad (ṢAAS)* stated: "Truthfulness leads to Al-Birr (righteousness) and Al-Birr (righteousness) leads to Paradise."[2] In the world of public policy and its implementation in Islam (that is a course of action or inaction undertaken by a public authority or authorities to address a public problem) truth is the Muslim's sacred pledge with the Qur'an as the barometer.

BASMA I. ABDELGAFAR
March, 2018

*(ṢAAS) – *Ṣallā Allāhu ʿalayhi wa sallam*: May the peace and blessings of God be upon him. Said whenever the name of the Prophet Muhammed is mentioned.

I
Introduction

1

Public Policy in Islam: A *Maqāṣid* Approach

> ... God has sent down the basic and fundamental principles, and left the interpretation and application of those principles to people's mental and intellectual capability of deduction, rationalization, and wisdom. It is people's responsibility to decide how to use God's revelation to serve the needs and interests of the human community.
>
> SHEIKH MUHAMMAD AL-GHAZALI[3]

This collection of chapters aspires to provide an introductory understanding of public policy in Islam and the *maqāṣid* approach by which anyone claiming an Islamic reference must govern. Public policies are instruments that define a course of action or inaction taken by authorities to address public concerns. When we qualify this definition with 'in Islam' we must propose the criteria that differentiate the discipline from its mainstream counterpart. Public policy in Islam is hereby defined as follows: A course of action or inaction undertaken by a public authority or authorities to address a public problem or challenge or to take advantage of an opportunity that (1) **is checked by Qur'anic morality and ethics as embodied in *taqwa* and *tawḥīd*;** (2) **justified by the higher objectives or *maqāṣid al-sharīʿah*; guided by** (3) **collective decision-making processes or *shūrā; and*** that (4) **results in reform and improvement or *iṣlāḥ*.** The *maqāṣid* or objectives of Divine law can be thought of as guiding principles for the determination of policy goals as well as the delimitation of the processes and substance of governance. Governance in Islam represents a serious responsibility given its impact on individuals, other living creatures, communities and the collective wellbeing of humanity. Its importance warrants a reconsideration of the hegemonic influence of traditional jurisprudence on political and policy studies in Islam that has had problematic implications for public authorities and citizens in predominantly Muslim societies as well as non-Muslim ones.

The distinctly *religious-legal* domination of the enterprise has been an inhibiting and divisive force within the Islamic world and between Islamic communities and others. Rigidity and legal hubris combined with a self-appointed guardianship of the faith amounted to rule by three proxies: the governing authorities; jurists and scholars; and the Muslim mind itself. This left little room for diversity, persuasion and collective goal determination and decision-making. Thus, the potential contribution of Islamic proposals in a competitive marketplace of policy ideas and alternatives has been greatly curtailed. Public problems tend to be viewed as legal questions, resolvable through the application of jurisprudence (fiqh) and the fundamentals of jurisprudence (*uṣūl* al-fiqh) of one or more of the conventional schools of law.[4] What could not be directly derived from explicit rulings (*aḥkām*) was relegated to the realm of unrestricted interests (*al-maṣāliḥ al-mursalah*) of which Shariʿah oriented-politics is an upshot. Through these fields of scholarship, purposefulness and dynamism have given way to the dictates of sociopolitical stability irrespective of injustice and clear violations of Islamic morality, objectives and pluralism.

Much of this legal hubris continues today in the persons and organizations that claim to represent Islam for major Muslim communities around the world. But over the last century important works and critiques have emerged regarding the robustness and universality of traditional scholarship including the extent of its utility in informing human advancement in the modern age. Though very much a part of Islam's intellectual heritage, the *maqāṣid* approach is considered a breakthrough in the field of Islamic jurisprudence, which clearly offers a roadmap for policy studies among other modern disciplines. Perceptive Muslim scholars have begun to highlight the role that the *maqāṣid* approach can play in matters of governance and public policy while remaining cognizant of the power of traditional jurisprudence and the influence of the religious establishment on matters of governance. We are gradually learning how to supplement religious-legal approaches with more comprehensive, purposeful, dynamic and complex modes for analyzing problems and proposing solutions while remaining true to Islam's primary sources, the Qur'an and Sunnah.

This introductory chapter presents the background behind my efforts. It is not intended to summarize the remaining chapters. Instead, it tells a story about the limits of the religious-legal approach that has dominated Islamic governance studies, about the way those limits have yet to be appreciated, about the way *maqāṣid* are stepping up to the challenge, and about the difficulties that lie ahead. Although different narratives may be valid, I do not believe that they do justice to the lived experience of Muslims around the world and the consequences they have suffered on account of the limits of the religious-legal approach and the unjustified deference that is broadly bestowed on our past. There is currently no persuasive account of our contemporary predicament in governance and public policy.

Shūrā

I start with the most glaring of all limits to the religious-legal approach to policy and politics. Despite the agreement of many renowned traditional jurists over the importance and necessity of *shūrā*,[5] commonly understood as consultation, in almost all spheres of life, the requirement that Islamic governance and policy be subject to such a process remains largely rhetorical. *Shūrā* is in fact more than consultation. It is a divinely ordained process of collective decision-making that derives its meaning from the world of honeybees. The literal definition of *shūrā* is the *extraction of honey from its source* alluding to the recommendation that any decision-making process and its outcomes must be illuminating and beneficial, i.e., lead to improvements (*iṣlāḥ*).

This message was clearly understood and applied by Abū Bakr, first caliph who insisted that governance, and people's affairs more broadly, must be managed through an understanding of public interests and a process of collective decision-making. He understood that the Qur'anic commandment to practice *shūrā* was meant to generate creative solutions to public problems and to resolve matters of disagreement by engaging stakeholders and ensuring public acceptance. Abū Bakr argued that differences of opinion were part of God's laws or *sunnan* and that the prioritization of some points of view over others was a natural outcome of the process of collective decision-making or *shūrā.*[6] Dispense fatwa or religious edicts as jurists will, public policy and public affairs demand a robust system of collective decision-making. The historical dismissal or devaluation of this process, despite its clear Qur'anic foundation, by certain jurists, scholars and political activists has distorted a major ordinance of good governance. According to *al-*Raysuni, "the functions and purposes that are fulfilled through consultation and for the sake of which consultation was established in Islam have generally been treated by Muslim scholars and writers in the most summary terms."[7]

The Qur'anic allusion to the animal kingdom when it comes to guiding human efforts concerning collective decision-making is highly significant and complex. There are two chapters in the Qur'an that help to explain the significance of this allusion, *al-Naḥl* (The Bees) and *al-Shūrā* (Collective Decision-Making).

In *al-Naḥl*, *shūrā* is contextualized within a complex reality that emphasizes the unity of design, which is revealed through Divine proofs that are expressed in the sacred texts and manifested in nature. Unravelling the intricate connection between these proofs, the values that they reveal, the objectives they guide toward and the universal laws they follow demands the application of intelligence at different levels of sophistication and the establishment of collective decision-making mechanisms that enable the pooling of human capacities, resources and spiritual insights for this purpose. The surah's appeal to the unity of all living matter is furthered by an account of how God inspired the bee to build its home in hills, trees, and in the habitations made by humans. Bees, we are told, are also inspired to eat from all the fruit, produce, flowers and plants, and to follow the ways that have been inspired to them by their Lord (*al-Naḥl*: 68-69). Indeed, modern science has revealed that *those ways* include a process of collective decision-making from which humans have much to learn as described below.

In *Surah al-Shūrā*, we are given a lengthy introduction to the inevitability of disagreements among people. This is not presented as an adverse condition of humanity but rather as a natural outcome of diversity and a necessary condition for successful collective decision-making. From this perspective, it is not our differences per se that are critical but rather the emphasis on our common interest. It is in the spirit of that common interest and the unity of design that as humans we must employ our diversity for our common good. It is important to note that 'our' in this context is not directed at Muslims exclusively but all people who respond to their Lord, establish prayer, conduct their affairs by *shūrā*, and give charity from what God has granted them to ease the lives of others. It therefore applies to all persons who can more or less uphold these principles and who lead moral lives.

The Revealed word, however, is not sufficient to fully explain the wisdom of the connection of *shūrā* to human decision-making. For that we must turn to the scientific literature which reveals the lessons that humans can learn from the collective decision-making process of honeybees. Based on the latest research, scientists are proposing that honeybees appear to have the best collective decision-making process on the planet. The obligation to practice *shūrā* can only be fully understood through an integration of the Revealed and unrevealed word.

In the Qur'an we are told that bees are Divinely inspired to search for and choose homes that best meet their survival criteria. These criteria are used to build consensus among a swarm of bees. Honeybees use a form of "direct democracy" to choose their new dwelling where individual bees participate directly rather than through representatives. Through open competition each participating bee presents (through dancing) its proposed alternative. The presentation demonstrates the extent to which that alternative meets the Divinely inspired criteria. In other words, each bee tries to persuade others of its alternative. Observers must make independent assessments of each proposal and decide whether to accept or reject. There is no blind followership since each bee can only support an alternative after independent investigation. As certain alternatives are increasingly endorsed they receive further support from others. Support for poorer alternatives gradually fades as the bees stop promoting them. Each bee thus remains a highly flexible participant in the decision-making process as its interest, like all others, is survival and its loyalty is directed toward settling on the best alternative. Scientific studies have greatly enhanced our awareness of why the Qur'an refers people to the world of honeybees to improve collective decision-making skills.

In Islamic scholarship, *shūrā* has been examined as both a principle as well as a decision-making process in governance as well as in other spheres of life. Much literature can be found on the relationship of *shūrā* to democracy though the Shariʿah does not support a particular political or voting system.[8] Nevertheless, the command to conduct affairs through *shūrā* has often been interpreted to mean "by some form of constitutional democracy."[9] To Kamali *shūrā* "is the Islamic equivalent of democracy but in comparison the latter is individualist in orientation, whereas *shūrā* is more community oriented for it contemplates consultative judgments and decisions, taken as a result of contact and association with those who may have something to say and an opinion to contribute." [10] Basically, *shūrā* "requires the head of state and government leaders to conduct community affairs through consultations with community members"[11] and does not preclude the choice of leadership itself. Every citizen who wishes to engage with public affairs must have the opportunity and security to do so regardless of religion or any other perceived difference.

Thus, some studies offer a similar understanding of *shūrā* as we now understand it from studying honeybees. Others fall short when making exceptions concerning its mandatory and binding nature, scope of use, and the overwhelming power of leadership, which does not conform to the model in nature. *Shūrā* is obligatory having been stated immediately after the injunctions to respond to God and to do Salah (42:38) (worship of God and prostration to Him through the five daily obligatory Prayers). Ibn Taymiyyah and Mohammad Abdu viewed *shūrā* as obligatory.[12] Al-Ṭabarī, even suggested that *shūrā* was one of the "fundamental principles of the Shariʿah (*ʿaẓā'im al-aḥkām*), which are essential to the substance and identity of Islamic government."[13] Al-Raysuni argues that *shūrā* is actually mandatory in all matters except those of a personal nature.[14] The Prophet himself was commanded by God to comply with *shūrā* (*Āl ʿImrān*: 159). Through the application of *shūrā*, Prophet Muhammad demonstrated that a leader's power, even if he be a prophet, must be limited and that the participation of concerned stakeholders in decision-making is mandatory.

What we know about *shūrā* today from the life of bees gives us a clear indication of the nature of the governance institutions that we

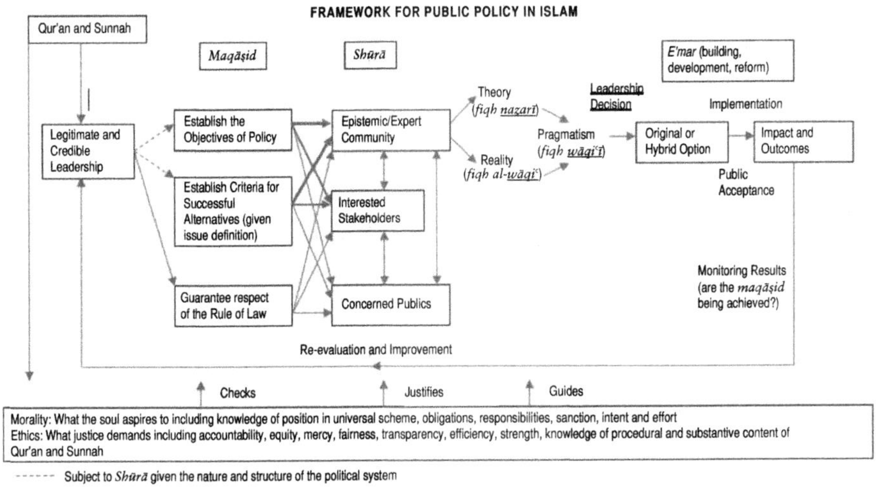

must develop so that public affairs are not only decided collectively but more significantly that they are decided in accordance with the public interest and the most advanced state of human knowledge concerning any specific issue. In a bee colony, the scout bees play an especially prominent role in searching for food and shelter. In other words, there is a group of worker bees whose primary task is to ensure the survival of the species through their ability to locate, assess and communicate their findings to others who naturally do not have the same inspiration, role or mobility. They do this against numerous and complex criteria.

In the human realm, *shūrā* is most suitably defined as a system of collective decision-making where public leaders draw upon epistemic communities who must engage the publics in an ongoing process of communication that seeks to solicit further input and/or garner support for the policy alternatives under consideration. This process is therefore most closely akin to management of public affairs through a system of expert advice that encompasses certain features. It involves leadership, expertise, civic participation, decision criteria, evidence, persuasion, investigation, voting/elections, quorum and consensus. Leadership in this system is important but it is not hegemonic. Leadership is primarily responsible for catalyzing processes that (1) solicit advice on problem definitions; (2) define criteria for successful outcomes; (3) propose possible responses; (4) persuade the public as to best course; and (5) give rise to the best collective decisions. The leader also heads the apparatus that implements policies and subsequently monitors, reviews and amends policies if outcomes are not satisfactory. Again, these functions may be subject to *shūrā* if they entail a significant change of course. Decisions based on *shūrā* appear to be time bound, lasting only as long as they produce their intended benefits.

In contrast to the individualistic and occasionally group nature of predominantly male dominated religious productions, an epistemic community "is a network of professionals with recognized expertise and competence in a particular domain and an authoritative claim to policy relevant knowledge within that domain or issue area."[15] It may consist of...

> professionals from a variety of disciplines and backgrounds, ... [who] have (1) a shared set of normative and principled beliefs, which provide value-based rationale for the social action of community members; (2) shared causal beliefs, which are derived from their analysis of practices leading or contributing to a central set of problems in their domain and which then serve as a basis for elucidating the multiple linkages between possible actions and desired outcomes; (3) shared notions of validity, that is, intersubjective, internally defined criteria for weighting and validating knowledge in the domain of their expertise; and (4) a common policy enterprise, that is, a set of common practices associated with a set of problems to which their professional competence is directed, presumably out of the conviction that human welfare will be enhanced as a consequence.[16]

As part of an Islamic rooted conception of *shūrā*, epistemic communities might imply groups of experts and professionals, not necessarily scientists, who are allied by a shared belief in *maqāṣid al-sharīʿah* and all the attendant implications of this belief on their thoughts and proposals. In other words, they must constantly be engaged in an intellectual movement between the signs or proofs in the written text and those manifested in nature, seeking guidance and evidence with the surety that the understanding of either cannot approach completeness without an understanding and exploration of the other. Their ultimate goal and challenge is the discovery of how governance decisions can best honour God's command to *join what must be joined* and to propose the boundaries where a community may justifiably define issues so that important decisions are not unduly hampered. In light of this, uncertainty takes on a whole new dimension compared with traditional jurisprudence.

The extent of our uncertainty is not limited to our experience with the texts but rather to our understanding of how the texts combine with the evidence we perceive in the universe to give meaning and truth to both. Levels of uncertainty are necessarily augmented by the reinforcing nature of what is written and what is observed. Epistemic communities must be expected not only to suggest "depictions of social or physical processes, their interrelation with other processes, and the likely consequences of actions that require considerable scientific or technical expertise"[17] but also to be willing and capable of integrating and relating such knowledge to the primary sources and particularly the Qur'an.

There is no question that epistemic community members' "understanding of the world and the formulation of alternative actions are shaped by belief systems, operational codes, and cognitive maps."[18] Auda similarly suggests that fiqh is an inherently cognitive exercise and that jurists are necessarily influenced in their perceptions, methods and pronouncements by a worldview.[19] In light of this, Ramadan proposes that introducing scholars of the 'context' may help augment the intellectual limitation of traditional jurists,[20] yet he is not sufficiently critical of the limitations of knowledge of the scholars of the context nor does he address the challenge that emerges on account of the fact that in today's world those who possess the most advanced state of knowledge do not likely profess Islam and as such do not perceive the value of resorting to the Qur'an. Because religion, even when it remains tacit, imposes 'cognitive restraints on rationality,'[21] it tends to play a stronger role than most people are willing to concede. This presents us with a dual challenge as both traditional jurists and scholars of the context ignore those dimensions of an issue that they cannot perceive or process as a result of established methodologies. In what follows we will see how the *maqāṣid* approach can help epistemic communities navigate this challenge even when members do not profess the same faith.

The proposals of any epistemic community or its individual members in the Qur'anic system of *shūrā* must be free of self-aggrandizement. The Qur'an states: "Nor walk on the earth with insolence: for you cannot penetrate the depths of the earth or reach the height of mountains" (*al-Isrā'*: 37). Measurability against pre-determined objectives or *maqāṣid* will help to control the likelihood of such tendencies. The power of persuasion necessary to carry leadership and interested actors from the broader community is the ultimate determinant of which proposals are acted upon. This ensures that the adoption of *shūrā* and its dependence on epistemic communities does not emerge as an elitist structure that is closed to public scrutiny and accountability. Each community must present the arguments that will carry other members of the community as well as interested members of the public who may similarly voice their opinions and concerns throughout the process, each with the right to vote for or against an alternative course. All strategic decisions must achieve quorum within an epistemic community before a final choice is made similar to the behavior of a honeybee swarm. The threshold of that quorum must be collectively determined while greater consensus must be achieved over time as a policy is implemented.

This system of decision-making accepts that leaders and other decision makers cannot possibly encompass all the complexities of an infinite number of public issues, nor are they expected to. In addition to the fact that this is not possible in public affairs with any degree of qualification, it guards against authoritarianism. By spreading responsibility, *shūrā* enhances the acceptance of decisions and outcomes among the electorate. A decision that is collectively negotiated and accepted gives rise to socially inclusive and resilient communities who are more willing to shoulder the consequences of actual outcomes. The leader from this perspective is responsible to the extent that she or he ensures that collective decision-making processes are ethically followed. For those endowed with mercy, justice, wisdom and intelligence this is a much more conducive system for self-accountability. In authoritarian settings the leader must and should bear the burden for his or her decisions. Irrespective of whether the outcomes are good or bad, such leaders will be held accountable for defying the mandatory Qur'anic injunction of *shūrā*.[22] The benefits of *shūrā* extend beyond actual government decisions and policies to stimulate social cohesion and communal responsibility, promote knowledge acquisition, specialization, cooperation, and so forth. Similarly, al-Raysuni suggests ten purposes and benefits of *shūrā* including: (1) determining the course of action which is correct, or the most correct; (2) release from the tyranny of subjectivity and selfish whims; (3) preventing high handedness and tyranny; (4) teaching humility; (5) giving everyone his due; (6) promoting an atmosphere of freedom and initiative; (7) developing the capacity for thinking and planning; (8) increased readiness for action and support; (9) promoting goodwill and unity; and (10) willingness to endure undesirable consequences.[23] In addition, it makes evidence and persuasion as opposed to narrow individual and group interests or undue historical reverence the focus of good decision-making.

Persuasion

Shūrā establishes that governance and policy cannot be subject to the issuance of fatwa or edicts by a group of predominantly male Muslim scholars let alone an individual. Persuasion is at the core of the *shūrā* process and indeed the message of Islam. The Qur'an challenges those who doubt to produce a surah (chapter) like that which it contains (*al-Baqarah*: 23) or to discover the truth by reflecting on the Qur'an itself (*Ṣād*: 29) and on the universe as evidence of its truth (*al-Baqarah*: 28-29). In communicating with the early recipients of the message, al-Ghazali explains: "*... the Qur'an adopted a rigorous, patient approach, amassing all possible evidence and using all methods of persuasion to make them see the truth* [emphasis added]."[24] Doubt and ignorance are no longer addressed by miracles and overt signs and more significantly must rely minimally on the instrument of command. Thus, we find that throughout the Qur'an rules are justified through values in an appeal to human reason.[25] In a knowledge-based society this approach should, at least in theory, be readily accepted.

The Qur'an came with an explicit message based on the power of reason. In fact, the commandment of reason is the only justified rule of conduct and legitimate authority. The Qur'an states: "Do they follow the command of their reason, or is it that they are an unjust people?"

(*al-Tur*: 32). Reason can only be exercised through all forms of literacy including reading, writing, numeracy and other forms of scientific learning. The Qur'an provides guidance on how people ought to "educate, instruct and argue."[26] God did not merely issue commands to people, since that would not have been effective in penetrating either the individual or collective consciousness. The Qur'an employs a number of tools to persuade, encourage and oblige the use of reason. Among others, these include comparisons to previous revelations (Torah and Gospel), storytelling, allusions, metaphors, repetition, challenges and appeals to the human senses, prospects of reward or punishment and dialogue. The latter is employed extensively in relaying the experiences of all the messengers for whom dialogue was the key approach with their followers, rejecters and notably with political authority.

The emphasis on persuasion reflects the importance that Islam places on 'carrying' concerned publics. The seriousness of the implications that Islam means for social, economic and political organization and structures demands considerable public support and engagement. Policies that promise to reform wealth distribution, class structures, equality of all forms and sexual norms are bound to suffer intense rejection. A considerable segment of Prophet Muhammad's community rejected Islam's message as was the case with the prophets that preceded him because of its implications for polity and economy. Even so, he was commanded to be patient and to continue to persuade people to accept Islam (*al-Anʿām*: 34) for the benefits that it introduces to their private and public lives, as individuals and communities, in this world and the next.

Prophet Muhammad had the unenviable task of persuading people to accept the Divine message without the supernatural manifestations that had for instance accompanied the messages of prophets Moses and Jesus. Islam was first and foremost a religion of reflection, observation and experimentation. It was a religion of persuasion and argument, proving the written word by evidencing the experiential world. The very first Qur'anic injunction to recite (*iqrā'*) "means the study, interpretation, and understanding of the principles, ideas and concepts that the Qur'an is putting forward."[27] Peoples demand for miracles (*al-Anʿām*: 7-8, *al-Ḥijr*: 7, *al-Isrā'*: 90-93) would no longer be delivered nor would the absolute command of authoritarian systems be entertained. Persuasion would be the only method from henceforth and the Prophet is told that no miracle would come from the heavens for the purpose of convincing humanity (*al-Anʿām*: 9) nor was he permitted to be an "autocrat over them" (*al-Ghāshiyah*: 22).

Throughout the Qur'an people are challenged to observe the beauty and order of the universe and everything in it while recognizing, as the Prophet reinforced, that we only experience glimpses into this natural reality (*al-Anʿām*: 104). Accepting this responsibility to explore and benefit from our understandings guarantees respect of the open and dynamic nature of Islam and ensures that every epoch identifies and develops the policies required to safeguard and enjoy life. The further away that we have moved from this perspective, the more intense our experience has become with injustice, wars, global warming, loss of biodiversity, global health epidemics, etc. The Qur'an tells us: "...God does not change the bounty with which He has graced a nation, until they have changed what is in their own selves, He is the hearer the knower" (*al-Anfāl*: 53). This effectively means that we are responsible for our own destiny. What we believe and how we behave ultimately impacts our reality.

The Qur'an suggests that our capacity to combine faith and knowledge in ways that serve humanity is the only way forward. The critical dimension of Islamic thought is to integrate all strands of knowledge – social and scientific – into an integrated whole and if that is not possible, which it is not, to try to mimic such unity to the greatest extent possible. Each generation is offered an incredible universe of discovery based on its prior achievements and preoccupations. With the knowledge of everything in the skies and on earth, God states that if all the trees on earth were pens, and the ocean was ink, even if extended sevenfold, His words would not be exhausted (*Luqmān*: 27). This has very profound meaning for the variety of ways in which humans can approach their social, scientific, economic, political and cultural challenges. Every interested and qualified individual and group should have the right to make contributions to this human journey. The only condition that Islam places on any contribution is that it must respect the unity and mutual interdependence of everything in the universe.

Social conduct and the protection of our environment are intimately interwoven in the narratives of the Qur'an. In the chapter of The Bees, verse after verse draws attention to the wonders of nature including the rain that gives us potable water and vegetation in all its splendor, all kinds of fruits, the sun, the moon, the stars, night and day, biodiversity, the seas and their diverse species from which we derive food and ornaments, the mountains and rivers, etc. All of this and much more are expressed as parts of a holistic system that points to the bounties of One Master (*al-Naḥl*: 10-17). In the following chapter, *Sūrah al-Isrā'* (The Night Journey), also known as *Sūrah Banī Isrā'īl* (The Children of Israel), verse after verse suggest the foundations of good social conduct. It includes worshiping one Lord, kindness to parents, duties toward kindred and strangers, exhortations to be generous but not to the point of excess, protection of children and family life, sanctifying life and restraint in times of loss, proper guardianship of orphans, fair trade, cautious followership, and humility.

The drive away from superstition, supernatural miracles and authoritarianism is foundational for public policy in Islam and good governance. Although Prophet Muhammad's mission was made more challenging by the fact that he had to rely on "persuasion, education, and reform alone,"[28] it was for our benefit and the long-term association of Islam with reason. How can people be persuaded to accept a certain course or action if the only way this could be accomplished was by absolute command and/or supernatural powers? Instead, invitation to the better way has to be through "wisdom and good counsel and stronger arguments" (*al-Naḥl*: 25).

The act of persuasion is not easy and indeed truthful advice may be a perilous exercise whether it is directed at those in authority or the general public from among which support and participation are sought. Prophet Muhammad had stressed the gravity of speaking truth to power when he characterized the act as the best of jihad.[29] The preservation of this ethic was explicitly respected during caliphates of Abū Bakr, ʿUmar and ʿAlī. The early caliphate was based on a contract between the ruler and ruled, where the ruler decreed that his rule was only valid so long as he upheld justice. These times are a far cry from the call of later jurists who "... in the interests of political stability...

demanded obedience to an unjust government which was in possession of military force..." The result was "political quietism" with the jurists "openly attempting to validate exercise of power in the interests of stability..."[30] This is a world where persuasion has no role and the sanctity of life is sacrificed for dubious interests. It is a position that defies the very essence of Islam and the Shariʿah the jurists claim to reference.

Speaking truth to power is a complex enterprise and requires activists and analysts to go beyond literal readings to understand the purposes of Qur'anic injunctions and their relation to and impact on the world given the relevant parameters of which they are aware. This demand necessitates a knowledge of *maqāṣid* or objectives of Divine law.

Maqāṣid

The argument for 'persuasion' in matters of governance as it clearly manifests itself in the Qur'an is impossible without a recognition of *maqāṣid* or objectives of Divine law (Shariʿah). The vast majority of rules in the Qur'an are justified in one way or another. Thus, to make amends with our *neighbors* is supported by the aphorism, "So make peace and reconciliation" (*al-Ḥujurāt*: 10). Likewise, to practice fair trade is justified with the statement, "that is better and gives the best result" (*al-Isrā'*: 35). This focus on purposes, objectives and intentions was not lost on the early caliphs.

The *maqāṣid* approach is commonly attributed to ʿUmar, the nascent community's second caliph. This is correct to the extent that ʿUmar put the approach to practice in all areas of governance though it was undoubtedly appreciated by Abū Bakr as well. Without a deep understanding of *maqāṣid*, ʿUmar would not have been able to administer and divide Muslim lands while creating of a number of government departments to organize the growing Muslim political body. In consultation with his advisors, he created numerous public institutions, guidelines and policies including an office of the ombudsman where residents of all lands under his authority could bring forward complaints against public officials. Moreover, he instituted strong anti-corruption and consumer protection policies by appointing officers to monitor, investigate and penalize illegal commercial activities. Notably, the first market inspector appointed in Madinah was a woman by the name of al-Shifā' bint ʿAbdullāh. Not only did she patrol the markets looking for any suspicious activity but also provided advice to merchants who were unsure of the permissibility of certain transactions.[31]

For ʿUmar rules existed to guide people under normal circumstances. All behaviors and decisions, whether rules-based or purpose-oriented, were guided by unyielding values and ethics. Compassion, transparency, equality, meritocracy, honesty, accountability, efficiency (perhaps to the point of austerity) and obedience strictly guided all matters related to the public service. This allowed ʿUmar to take a problem and context oriented approach to policy. His approach ushered an era of innovation in governance and public service. By observing what neighboring nations were doing, his rule saw the professionalization of defense, spread of education, health, welfare, and the creation of a central treasury and its provincial counterparts. It is evident that the *maqāṣid* orientation pervaded all of ʿUmar's governance decisions.

The exact details of the institutions that ʿUmar created and nurtured are not our concern. It is sufficient to recognize that these political, economic and social innovations were not detailed in the Qur'an. Instead, ʿUmar relied on his understanding of the purposes of Qur'anic injunctions. There are several well-documented occasions where ʿUmar took decisions that on their surface actually appeared to defy literal expressions in the Qur'an. For instance, he refused to distribute conquered lands as 'spoils of war' so as to not allow Muslims to dominate wealth and control massive swathes of land as well as non-combatant populations. He instituted a moratorium on the punishment for theft during the famine of Madinah insisting that the prioritization of life necessitated all measures.[32] In another instance, he declined to pay support to new converts to Islam despite the Qur'anic injunction to do so, asserting that this was only required when Islam was weak.[33] He also initiated a policy where a person's guild as opposed to their next of kin could pay the blood money in cases of accidental homicide.[34] In sum it is clear that ʿUmar used his understanding of the objectives of the Shariʿah or *maqāṣid* to rule with justice and equity. His pioneering spirit and confidence challenges all contemporary positions that Islam does not permit or encourage innovation in public policy and governance.

Despite its early expressions in matters of governance, the formal elaboration of the *maqāṣid* approach did not occur until the tenth century. It was then that a select group of Muslim jurists appealed to the idea to exhort their contemporaries to heed the objectives of the Shariʿah in making legal pronouncements and interpreting the texts. The superficial limits that had been placed on the understanding of the Shariʿah and what it actually encompassed by authoritarian rulers as well as self-censored scholars had confined Islam's intended contribution to political, social and economic reform and renewal.

With great ambition, the early aim of the *maqāṣid* approach was to unify the body of fiqh or jurisprudence that was already in existence and to insist that future productions respected an ethical framework that scholars could agree upon. The approach's founding fathers also sought to encourage the lay believer to recognize that Islamic law aimed at achieving benefits and preventing harms. The *maqāṣid* provided a guide for scholars and lay people alike. By "elucidating the objectives of Islam, the causes behind Islamic legal rulings as well as the intentions and goals which underlie the Shariʿah, or Islamic Law, they made it clear that every legal ruling in Islam has a function which it performs, an aim which it realizes, a cause, be it explicit or implicit, and an intention which it seeks to fulfill and all of this in order to realize benefit to human beings or to ward off harm or corruption."[35] Several prominent jurists even suggested that the *maqāṣid* should take on the fixed and obligatory nature of the fundamentals of jurisprudence or *uṣūl*. For this group of theorists, the main purpose of the *maqāṣid* was not only to demonstrate that all juridical productions aimed at achieving the higher objectives of the Shariʿah as described by the approach but also to reject those productions that could not achieve this connection.

In its traditional form, the *maqāṣid* approach focuses on the preservation of what the scholars termed the six objectives or essentials. These objectives coincide with what the early scholars perceived as the positive dimensions of the legal limits in the penal code. Thus, they posited that Islamic law promoted benefits and prevented harm by preserving religion, life, mind, progeny, wealth and dignity. Al--Shāṭibi (d. 1388) went so far as to maintain that the law was laid down for no other purpose than to preserve these six essentials or interests[36] and, as a result, all specific rules have to yield to their priority.[37] This view is widely shared by contemporary scholars of *maqāṣid* who see these six principles as the "unchangeable core of all religions and legal systems."[38] The ultimate goal of these scholars is to see the six objectives emerge as the "unshakeable foundations for every act of *ijtihad* and for all Islamic thought."[39]

The *maqāṣid*, even in their traditional format, provide important direction for public policy and governance. To have as paramount ends the advancement of life, dignity, faith, intellect, progeny, and wealth is to challenge policy development and implementation every step of the way and to question the intents and contributions of stakeholders and other interested parties. The conventional vision of the legal-religious approach can only ever be a limited player in this much more democratic and accountable process. This is a universal approach that invites the engagement of people from all walks of life and systems of belief. It is one that distinguishes between ethics and religion for the greater good of humanity.

Ethics and Religion

A distinction must be made between ethics and religion for public policy and governance in Islam to be a universal enterprise. We already saw how the model for collective decision-making is actually derived from the animal kingdom removing any objection to its potentially religious association, except for the Muslim belief that bees are ultimately inspired by God. Indeed, the Qur'an is replete with such allusions and other methods that demand the use of reason if we are to fully appreciate their wisdom and utility. Knowledge derived from the Qur'an is fundamentally ethical though not unconditionally religious.

There is no more a brilliant explanation for this than in the 1947 doctoral work of Sheikh Mohammed Abdallah Draz.[40] Qur'anic ethics, he explains, cannot be considered religious without qualification. First, he points to the comprehensiveness of the Qur'an and the fact that it covers every facet of life in one way or another. In contrast, the religious element, which involves worship, is not only limited but intensely personal. Second, it is clear to see that the proposed ethics are verified in this very life through human conscience, legal power and the prerogative that every human being strives toward the promotion of good and prevention of evil. Third, the Qur'an does not primarily or mostly rely on fear and hope to justify its rules but rather demands the attention, comprehension and advancement of human reason. In this way it does not only suit individuals with different capacities but more critically leads and responds to changes in time and space.

This is not to say that religion plays no role. I have already noted the role that beliefs play in shaping the approach, values, definitions and hence proposals of epistemic communities. Religion undoubtedly plays a role in organizing and guiding our thoughts and actions. This does not mean, however, that ethics and religion define each other. In existential terms, reason came before the positive law of religion.[41] Right and wrong are inspired to every soul at its creation. It is through reason that we shape and accept both religious and natural law. Neither is imposed on the conscience without its acknowledgement.[42] Finally, it is important to note that religious rules only offer a contribution to the formulation of a starting point toward decision-making. Every individual or group of individuals will necessarily be constrained by capacity, limits to knowledge and other circumstances. Thus, even with the acceptance of religious rules we must still determine our own course of action and its purpose or *maqṣid* at any given point in time given the other parameters that define the needs of a situation.

Religion becomes a factor only when we consider intentionality, the realm in which the believer attempts to align their will with that of God. In other words, it is the intentions behind any act that render it religious whether expressed as pure devotion or social activity. As such, its explicit manifestation is almost impossible and can in no way be imposed on others or even expected of them. Not only has the Qur'an made this manifestly clear by stating that there is no compulsion in religion (*al-Baqarah*: 256) but it also stated: "You cannot guide [to faith] those you love; but God guides [to faith] whom He pleases; and He knows best those who are guided" (*al-Qaṣaṣ*: 56). This is a further confirmation for believers to eschew any pretense of this capacity or desire. Moreover, the Qur'an also commanded Muslims to respect the rituals of others.

Faith is a personal and voluntary choice. There is no compulsion in matters of belief. Freedom of conscience is an inviolable right in Islam whether we are talking about personal choice or public governance. Those who choose to believe, however, cannot be contented with their inner development only. Every command to have faith in the Qur'an is accompanied with a command to perform good and beneficial works.[43] A believer is tested in this sincerity through witnessing the needs and realities of life, circumstances that by virtue of their claim to belief they cannot ignore. Even in circumstances where there is no dire necessity for action, a believer is commanded to promote life in its full colors, to advance humanity and discover the truths that deepen our faith and guide our engagement with an ever-complex world.

Mercy Versus Justice

The Shari^cah's emphasis on pluralism and peace highlights a subtle but critical difference between the ultimate ethical value of the legal-religious approach and that of the *maqāṣid* as applied to Islamic governance and policy. The nature of the law and its principles predisposes Islamic scholars to prioritize the concept of justice in their thoughts and outputs. Justice is primarily concerned with fair and equal treatment in accordance with the Qur'an and Sunnah. In her book on Islamic jurisprudence, al-Hibri argues that "the centerpiece of the Islamic worldview is *ʿadālah*, or Divine justice."[44] Kamali confers by stating that "a fundamental aim of the shari'ah is to implement justice (*ʿadl* or *qisṭ*) and promote benefits (*maṣāliḥ*) to humans."[45] For the Shariah Index Project (SIP), justice "is the foundational principle of Islamic governance."[46] The purpose of justice, according to Abdul Rauf, "is the appearance of unity... justice allows for people to come together in concord and peace, rather than as antagonistic parties vying over their respective interests."[47] Broadening on this theme, Auda explains: "I understand the 'Islamic law' to be a drive for a just, productive, developed, humane, spiritual, clean, cohesive, friendly, and highly democratic society."[48]

The extension of the *maqāṣid* approach to governance, however, cannot adopt this perspective uncritically. Even as a principle of Islamic law, the Prophet had warned: "It is fairer for the judge to err in acquittal than in conviction."[49] In other words, tending toward mercy is a higher value than trying to achieve justice when there is doubt. Nevertheless, judging between people in court is a very different task than governing communities at different administrative levels.

It ought to be indisputable that Islamic governance and its associated policies are unabashedly and explicitly concerned with mercy. Prophet Muhammad had said: "Show mercy to everything on earth so that He in the heavens will have mercy on you."[50] He also said: "May the mercy of God be on one who is kind and forbearing when he sells, kind and forbearing when he buys, and kind and forbearing when he makes a demand."[51] Compassion, understanding, forgiveness and pardon are the hallmarks of Divine governance and the ethical values that are intended to reign strict application of the word of the law. I do not believe that any credible jurist or scholar of Islam, including those referred to above, would deny this assertion though they may not prioritize it. Indeed, every scholar admits that mercy is the most salient of God's attributes and as such the defining characteristic of His rule. Thus, Kamali succinctly states:

> The Qur'an explicitly states that its *raison d'être* is to bring mercy and serve as a "healing to the (spiritual) ailment of the hearts, guidance, and mercy (*raḥmatan*) for the believers" (10:57). Likewise, it asserts that the most important purpose of Prophet Muhammad's prophethood is to provide mercy: "We have not sent you but as a mercy (*raḥmatan*) to the worlds (*li al-ʿālamīn*)"(21:107). In its plural form, "worlds" implies that God's mercy is boundless. It extends to the entirety of humanity and even beyond to the animal world and other worlds we may not know. This emphasis on mercy is conveyed explicitly when God declares, "My *raḥmah* extends to all things" (*wa raḥmatī wasiʿat kulla shay'*) (7:156). The central role of mercy is also apparent in the fact that of Gods ninety-nine beautiful names (*al-asmā' al-ḥusnā*), the two names that introduce 113 of the 114 chapters of the Qur'an are *al-Raḥmān* (Most Beneficent) and *al-Raḥīm* (Most-Merciful)...[52]

In fact, the more apt translation of *al-Raḥmān al-Raḥīm* is the Merciful, the Giver of Mercy, which further emphasizes this characteristic of Divine rule. Both words in Arabic emanate from the same root *ra-ḥa-ma* and it is important to translate them as such to demonstrate more effectively how the Divine places utmost importance on this name and attribute.

The seriousness of this value premise for governance and policy from an Islamic perspective cannot be understated. In fact, each and every one of us is physically and morally bound by this value premise. The Qur'an tells us: O people, be cognizant of your Lord who created you from one being (*nafs*) and from her created her mate and propagated from them many men and women, and be mindful of God by whom you entreat [each other], and the wombs (*al-arḥām*), surely God is your overseer (*al-Nisā'*: 1). The 'being' referred to in this verse is the *Raḥīm*, a Qur'anic term for which the English translation of 'womb' is meaningless. In a sacred narration or *ḥadīth qudsī*, we are told that it is God, *al-Raḥmān*, who named The Womb *al-Raḥīm* stressing both the physical and moral imperative of mercy among humankind as it is our common source. In it He declares: "I am The Merciful, I created the *Raḥīm* and cleaved her a name from my name, so whoever keeps connected with her, I will connect with him and whoever severs ties with her, I will sever My ties with him."[53] This sacred narration and the verse noted above from the Qur'an are mutually confirming. All people are commanded to be heedful of their Lord and the wombs, *al-arḥām,* that bore them and that connect them to the original source. Understood both factually and figuratively, *al-arḥām* are connected to the mother of all wombs, *al-Raḥīm,* that was the source of all humanity and to whom God had made a promise only to keep ties with those who keep ties with her.

The *Raḥīm* represents both the physical and moral connection of humanity. Physically every person is related to every other person through our original connection to the *Raḥīm*. Although some scholars limit this relation to perceivable family, I believe that it encompasses all of humanity as every source of human propagation is necessarily connected to the original source. The nature of these physical relations that we are commanded to sanctify is determined by the moral attribute of the source, which we are told is a direct derivation from The Merciful. In other words, we must not only treat each other with mercy but we must reflect this moral imperative in all our human endeavors. This is the definition of heedfulness toward God, and heedfulness toward *al-arḥām*.

A *maqāṣid* approach to governance is explicitly normative by embracing without hesitation the moral imperative of mercy above all other value premises. As such it is also prescriptive in recommending the values that must override others when governing and formulating policy. Governance from an Islamic reference is first and foremost about holistic human welfare. Justice is important, a very close second, but it does not capture the most profound essence of Islamic governance and indeed it scarcely suffices for Islamic law. We say scarcely because although the Qur'an clearly espouses concepts of justice and equity, it immediately follows these with the excellence of forgiveness, pardon, generosity and beauty, all elements of mercy. For example, in the case of murder, believers are commanded to apply *qiṣāṣ*. This concept has been variously explained as the law of equality or retaliation in kind, i.e., life for life. But neither explanation captures the full meaning of the Qur'anic concept that emphasizes the possibility of pardon and reciprocation of generosity and goodwill in such cases. We are told that in *qiṣāṣ* there is the preservation of a life as a concession and *mercy* from God (*al-Baqarah*: 178-179).

Moreover, Prophet Muhammad had said: "He who does not show mercy, will not be shown mercy"[54] and it was revealed to him to command people to dispense mercy (*al-Baqarah*: 219). This becomes particularly evident in the area of governance. When the Prophet sent two governors to Yemen he exhorted them to: "Facilitate things for the people and do not make things difficult for them. Be kind and lenient [both of you] with the people, and do not be hard on them and give the people good tidings and do not reject them."[55] This approach would be followed by all four rightly-guided caliphs. The last of whom was ʿAlī ibn Abī Ṭālib who similarly advised his governor of Egypt, which had a large Christian population:

> Infuse your heart with mercy, love and kindness for your subjects. Be not in the face of them a voracious animal, counting them as easy prey, for they are of two kinds: either they are your brothers in religion or your equals in creation. Error catches them unaware, deficiencies over-

come them, [evil deeds] are committed by them intentionally and by mistake. So grant them your pardon and your forgiveness to the same extent that you hope God will grant you His pardon and forgiveness. For you are above them, and he who appointed you is above you, and God is above him who appointed you.

It is clear that mercy is the defining feature of *maqāṣid*-based governance and those aspiring to contribute to this field must not only acknowledge this but also have the capacity to incorporate its meaning in their research, advice and activism. This moral imperative has to be reflected in our institutions and in the ways we run them. Action and outcomes are central features of Islam so that translating mercy into what we do, rather than merely what we say, becomes the *maqāṣid* approach's distinguishing mark both from traditional jurisprudence and also from non-Islamic policy studies. To err on the side of mercy can only result in beneficial outcomes both for the incumbent government and its leaders, and the societies they govern.

Challenges of a Nascent Discipline

Applying the *maqāṣid* approach to governance and public policy is a new enterprise and this comes with certain challenges. In the first instance it must overcome the hurdles erected by a deeply entrenched religious-legal paradigm, which insists that the Shariʿah has little to say on state affairs. But it must also challenge contemporary *maqāṣid* scholars who simply shift the *maqāṣid* framework from jurisprudence to governance and policy without qualification and without having reconstructed the edifice that would make this possible in a way that ensures clear reference to the primary sources.

One of the most serious fallacies that we must debunk is that the Shariʿah has little or nothing to say about the nature of the state. Many contemporary scholars claim that the Shariʿah is silent concerning the state. Part of the confusion is due to a conflation of the Shariʿah or Divine law with fiqh or jurists understanding of that law. Fiqh refers to "the huge collection of juridical opinions that were given by various jurists from various schools of thought, in regards to the application of Shariʿah to their various real life situations throughout the past fourteen centuries."[56] This collection is predominantly based on *āyāt al-aḥkām* or the legislative verses of the Qur'an totaling about 250 of 6000 verses and about 1200 *aḥādīth al-aḥkām* or Prophetic narrations with legislative content.[57] Collectively, these Qur'anic verses and narrations are commonly but mistakenly referred to as the Shariʿah though it is clear that they can only ever comprise a very small segment of it.

Even a cursory study of the Shariʿah reveals that politics and policy are important foci of Qur'anic rules and narratives. Flexibility regarding the exact form of state authority does not negate its existence or the provision of every element required to build a robust system. The Qur'an unequivocally states that not a single thing has been neglected in the Book (*al-Anʿām*: 38). The observation by Kamali that the Shariʿah "does not convey a great deal of awareness about state authority and the political interests of its agencies and institutions"[58] betrays the numerous references and narratives within the Qur'an where elements of state authority are clearly manifest. Abu Ridah likewise erroneously states: "One cannot help but note the absence of the notion of the state which possesses authority and which guards and implements the religion, and this inspite of its appearance in the writings of ethicists..."[59] What these and many other scholars are referring to is a historical construction as embodied in fiqh, not the Shariʿah, which is the guidance variously presented in the unchanging expanse of Divine law.

Restricting the understanding of the Shariʿah has disabled policy experts from mining the Qur'an for invaluable content relating to both processes and substance. A strong historical legacy that extolled the virtues of separating Islamic affairs from governance in the name of stability and obedience resulted in the false acceptance that the Shariʿah had nothing to say about state authority and state-citizen relations. In reality, it is the jurists that steered clear of the subject as a result of self-interest and censorship but also as a response to strict state directives. Yet it is clearly through studying the Shariʿah that democratic principles and the criteria of *shūrā* discussed above can be brought to the fore and implemented thereby addressing issues like tyranny, poverty and corruption.

This initial fallacy led to another fallacy which is the invention of a concept that would allow scholars and jurists to go beyond what they did not immediately perceive given the artificially imposed limits on the texts. 'Unrestricted interests' are rules and pronouncements "which are recognized by Islamic Law but which are not mentioned by name in any of the particular legal texts."[60] The concept is used to compensate for the limits of analogical reasoning[61] and justify productions related to the *maqāṣid* and *siyāsah sharᶜīyyah*. Yet it is an unnecessary classification if the shackles of fiqh and *uṣūl al-fiqh* are removed when we study the Shariᶜah (not fiqh) for policy and governance purposes. In fact, this is the only way that the *maqāṣid* approach can build a robust edifice to support such studies.

As opposed to unrestricted interests, *maqāṣid* for governance and policy requires development and reliance upon a new toolkit of methodologies for understanding the primary sources. Even a cursory consideration of Divine methodologies presented in the Qur'an reveals a wealth of techniques including dialogue, storytelling, example, information, exhortation, observation, allusion, metaphors, repetition, rulings (permissions and prohibitions), proofs, dialogue, etc. These methods can be applied within broader thematic, systems and cyclical approaches to the texts and the universe to which they apply. Thematic exegeses approach the Qur'an as an integral whole "looking for themes across its entirety, its chapters, and groups of verses" in stark contrast with traditional exegetes who put all their emphasis on the explanation of single words or verses.[62] Theme-based hermeneutics serve "to identify the basic theories and principle conceptualizations that represent the Islamic perspective. Rather than being content with nothing but superstructures and detailed legislation, this approach promises to make it possible to formulate a set of concepts which constitute a universal, cohesive system."[63]

A systems approach emphasizes the need to understand how the diverse elements in the primary sources, both physical and abstract, impact one another within their explicit or implicit contexts. The idea is to understand how the Divine design of systems gives rise to certain patterns that are different from the individual parts or even a subset of those parts. This latter kind of thinking eliminates the possibility of cherry picking from the Shariᶜah with the pretense that beneficial outcomes will necessarily be achieved. Systems thinking demands an acceptance of purposefulness, holism, openness, dynamism, and multi-dimensionality to mention only a few criteria.

Cyclical analysis involves studying the events recounted in the Qur'an both as narratives but also those which are revealed in fact format that present sufficient historic regularity that they can be forecasted into the future. There is no doubt that the information provided in the Qur'an is both relevant and reliable for this task though the aid of historical and other disciplinary contributions is necessary to suggest detailed and robust scenarios. Thus, analysis based on the Qur'an may yield important insights into the probability of repeated events and the factors that expedite or delay certain intervals.

Developing a new toolkit for the policy sciences will not be easy or expedient but it is a critical task. The consistent fallback of Islamic scholars and their students on traditional jurisprudence defeats the applicability of their ultimate proposals for modern policy and governance. The claim that the Shariʿah says nothing or very little about state authority and institutions must be rejected, while the concept of 'unrestricted interest' must be challenged. Such thinking only presents policy analysts with two extreme poles. Either we accept the micro, detailed, mundane and fragmented world of jurisprudence, or the relatively open and unhindered world of unrestricted interests. Reality and legitimacy inevitably rest on a spectrum somewhere between these two poles. It will be the challenge of those who see the middle ground to articulate and present alternatives.

Conclusion

This chapter highlighted the critical pillars of public policy in Islam. *Shūrā* imposes a collective decision-making process on public policy. In its absence, proper policy making cannot thrive as authoritarian contexts impede diversity and stifle dissent. Resilience is achieved when the policy process is receptive to expert advice that is obligated to fully investigate matters and persuade others of its robustness. The *maqāṣid* clarify the ends or objectives to which any policy alternative aspires and the extent to which it fulfills divinely inspired criteria. The ethical parameters presented in the Shariʿah are not intended for Muslims only, but those notions of peace and ethics are to be extended to all humanity, and indeed have universal appeal being valued and sought by almost everyone.

The Qur'an's emphasis on mercy makes this value the overriding concern of public policy in Islam. This does not diminish the professionalism or objectivity of the enterprise but rather it accepts that policy making is intrinsically value-laden. Those involved in policy are ultimately answerable to God. Their duty is most safely guarded when they advocate not only what is just and right, but what is merciful and equitable. Their vocation is not to play into the hands of human power, but to reform and balance it with the highest value expressed by Divine power. In short, their proposals cannot deviate from the Divine command of mercy.

For the *maqāṣid* approach to admit these concerns and thereby impact public policy and governance it will not only have to show relevance, but it will have to find those who are willing to develop, disseminate and defend its core premises. This is a challenging but not impossible task. Accepting the *maqāṣid* approach to open up the study of public policy in Islam is an important if only first step. The *maqāṣid* approach was not envisioned and developed for this purpose. Even so, several contemporary scholars have noted the approach's potential contribution to governance and policy among other disciplines. The chapters in this book aim to highlight key concerns and contributions.

2

Muslims and the Dilemmas of Governance

This Qur'an is a script encased within two covers, it does not speak, but rather it is men who speak with its knowledge.

ʿALĪ IBN ABĪ ṬĀLIB[64]

Islam is a global religion although it is often reduced to the history and culture of the Arabs and the geography of the Middle East. This association is understandable given the location of the religion's two holiest sites in addition to a number of other factors that include the birthplace of the Prophet of Islam, the language of the Qur'an, the scholastic hegemony of early scholarship, the location of several of the major centers of learning, as well as the focus of recent political struggles. Contemporary global interests and politics that seek to confine the *natural* place of Islam to the Arab world have leveraged these factors to further this stereotype. They have been aided in this effort by the highly dramatic events of the recent wave of protests in the Middle East that brought Islamist political parties to the fore in a number of Arab countries and a global media that reinforces cultural images of Islam in public perceptions.

In reality, Islam is the religion of over 1.7 billion people worldwide. The Middle East is home to only 20% of Muslims, about 62% live in South and South East Asia, 15% in Sub-Saharan Africa and there are sizeable minorities in the Americas, Europe, China and Russia. The presence of Muslims in these lands is sometimes due to recent waves of immigration, but in many instances is centuries old due to Islam's early expansion expeditions. Improvements in transportation and information and communication technologies have led to unprecedented personal and impersonal interactions among Muslims around the world. This ongoing and growing contact has had contradictory implications. While reviving the perception of the universalism of Islam with its great diversity, it has also intensified political competition among major Muslim states to control or dominate foreign populations and Islamic groups both culturally and politically. The success of these forces in overriding local cultures, that ought to be equally if not superiorly valid in interpreting Islam for local consumption, has been bolstered by the historically fortified relationship of Muslims to authority.

This chapter argues that today's Muslims appear to be ruled by three *authoritative* proxies over which they exercise limited control, whether through disinterest or caution. These include the state, irrespective of its system of governance; the traditional religious establishment of jurists, scholars and imams; and finally, by a generally distorted conscience that is convinced of its inability to independently ascertain the content of its beliefs without the guidance and intervention of external authority. Collectively, these three proxies including the ways in which they interact, represent the challenge that Muslims must overcome if they are to fulfill the approach to governance that is elaborated in the Shariʿah and honor the Divinely ordained diversity of humanity.

As a scene setter, this chapter is intended to offer a brief explanation of the governance dilemmas that Muslims face today. It is not a systematic or historical overview or a dedicated critique of other claims. In that way, it is a much more modest ambition that aims to highlight critical areas of concern and action. The historical notes provide a summary of my perspective on the relationship between rulers, scholars and the public. Theories that posit a golden era in Islamic governance which privileged the Shariʿah lead us to expect better outcomes than is currently evident, and as such are not equipped to explain ruptures with past experience. Such ruptures reflect ideological, institutional and psychological factors, which combined to subjugate the ummah[65] both to foreign forces but even much earlier to rulers who feigned an Islamic veneer.

To this end, the chapter is divided into four main parts. The first section, offers a brief historical perspective. The aim is to demonstrate that the arms-length relationship between governing authorities and their subjects during Islam's dynastic phase betrayed the precepts of the Shariʿah while nurturing the conditions that would eventually lead to the defeat of the ummah. The second, third and fourth sections then consider the ways in which the three authoritative proxies of state, religious establishment and self, have been shaped and perceived as a result of this process.

Historical Perspective

Historically, Muslim governance by dynastic rule and tribal loyalties created a dissonance between subjects and rulers. Starting from the seventh century, the nature of the relationship that emerged between the people and the rulers of the various dynasties was moderated by the religious establishment that largely perceived and therefore constructed Islamic jurisprudence with an almost exclusive individualistic and private bias. As a result, rulers were spared an elaboration and imposition of those aspects of the Shariʿah that defined good governance including the obligatory injunction of civic engagement, the right of civil disobedience when governing authorities are corrupt and an inviolable conception of human rights. By strictly defining the fundamentals of jurisprudence, albeit with some variations among the major schools, while delimiting the possibility of holistic reference to the Shariʿah, and in particular, respect of the entire Qur'anic text, the jurists absolved the rulers (and themselves) of direct responsibility for the governance conundrum that Muslims have suffered for centuries. Thus, modes of governance and public policies did not violate the Shariʿah as defined and understood by the jurists allowing contemporary scholars like Hallaq to argue credibly that the premodern era was characterized by a Shariʿah paradigm and that there was a clear separation of powers.[66] In reality, this separation was only possible because the jurists, both through the imperative of dynastic rule but also self-censorship, confined the Shariʿah within unjustifiable boundaries.

A strong religious establishment that exercised local control while insulating governing authorities created the façade of a dominant religious paradigm. This was perhaps the most conducive approach for facilitating the ever expanding ambitions of the Arab dynasties that emerged after the caliphate of Imam ʿAlī (d. 661). To deny that it also facilitated the subjugation of Muslims is to misunderstand the substance and processes of governance throughout Muslim history. Similarly, to lay unqualified blame on colonialism or the specificities of the modern state for our governance dilemmas today overlooks the role played by Muslims – rulers, jurists, activists and ordinary folk alike – in the making of history. That today's modern predicament is not of our making, as Hallaq contends, is to avoid responsibility and worse yet misunderstand or ignore how we got to where we are.[67]

Even lay observers would concede that the general historical trend that has seen power diffuse from central authorities, whether at the level of the family, community, nation or ummah or whether in the realm of civil society, business or government, to the individuals and groups that comprise these social entities has eluded many predominantly Muslim societies. The exercise of authority throughout societies where Islam is the dominant religion does not appear to have been sufficiently and positively influenced by economic growth and changing value systems. Muslim countries continue to have high rates of illiteracy, poverty, maternal mortality and human subjugation. They stand out in their disproportionate suffering from corruption, gender inequality, injustice, tyranny and violence. Despite sporadic and often violent attempts to join the global *democracy* bandwagon, these societies often find themselves thrust in even deeper authoritarianism, oppression and instability. These characteristics appear to carry over, albeit in milder forms, in other settings where Muslims are not necessarily surrounded by authoritarian, patriarchal and undemocratic political and cultural influences.

Modern forms of governance, and particularly the acceptance and facilitation of civic engagement, that have wrested legislative powers from religious establishments, monarchies, dictatorships, and military regimes elsewhere in the world, have eluded the vast majority of predominantly Muslim societies. That this has occurred through the propagation of the fiction of Divine sovereignty in matters of worldly governance is outlandish. The outcome has been a politically stagnant ummah, unduly swayed by political interests and divisions, vulnerable to entrapment by zealots, both religious and political, and incapable of distinguishing and sometimes not even aware of when, how and by whom our beliefs were hijacked. These are not challenges of modernity, they are consequences of our own history, culture, capabilities and choices. Most distinctly they are a consequence of the practice and perceptions of authority within the Muslim world.

The relatively restricted relationship of Muslims to different forms of authority that is reinforced by historical, cultural and misguided religious imperatives, coupled with a stagnant intellectual establishment that refuses to see the damage it has created, has facilitated Muslim subjugation and complacency around the world. The politically convenient demarcation that dynastic rule imposed between the jurists and rulers, had a significant impact on the productions and pronouncements of the former who were in large measure coopted by the authorities. It also nurtured an environment where religious scholars increasingly distinguished themselves and their enterprise from everyday believers. Gradually, religious education would come to reflect this distinguished status by providing suitable instruction only for those adopting religion as a vocation. Ordinary Muslims were compelled to rely on these individuals who over time became almost exclusively male for all affairs where religious guidance was perceived as necessary.

Authority of the State

For twelve centuries prior to colonialist rule, Muslims had become accustomed to a certain distance from governing authorities. They had accepted the myth of the 'silence' of the Shariʿah on matters of governance except for the unqualified demand for tribal allegiance. Islam ruled in their personal lives and even then, mostly in times of conflict. The acceptance by governing authorities of this arrangement gave an air of religious legitimacy to their rule. The rule itself with few exceptions, however, was as far from the Shariʿah as the subjects of authority were from authority.

The fiction of Divine sovereignty in matters of worldly governance deluded the Muslim masses. While God's sovereignty is indisputable in governing creation, it does not express itself in the details of our daily lives where we act of our own volition. Hence, the belief and propagation that God is the only source of law is not only erroneous it is dangerous. God's sovereignty is indisputable in the laws that govern creation. No human can alter these laws or the consequences of breaking them (*al-Rūm*: 30). Understanding, articulating and expressing the Shariʿah, however, is a human endeavor. When human beings undertake these efforts in any leadership capacity they cannot claim to be representing God. As Draz rightly notes, when we act we do so of our own volition, not as instruments of God, since there is no way of knowing His Divine will in advance. This is why the Qur'an proclaims our responsibility before God while it seemingly subordinates human to Divine will.[68]

Historically, the caliph or sultan was erroneously recognized as God's viceroy on earth to whom allegiance was owed by virtue of this representation. The oath of allegiance, however obtained, meant that the ruler enjoyed popular support. To betray the ruler meant a betrayal of Divine authority as well as the popular will. Although beliefs have since evolved especially during the past century with the emergence of 'political' Islam as the opposition, this has not rectified the belief that man is God's representative on earth or in some extreme cases that God is the sole legislator. This, despite the fact that the Qur'an is very clear about the separation of power and piety. Authority is often commanded by fallible and corrupt individuals and groups. Dynastic rule throughout Muslim history is no exception. Certain tribes amassed and concentrated power and wealth through murder and mischief behaviors that persist to date in certain political systems. Even when the Abbasid Empire replaced that of the Umayyads in 750 CE, bringing with them a greater sense of equality among their subjects, the upper echelons of government remained closed to the vast majority.

Without heeding the Qur'anic message of the processes and substance of good governance, or even respecting the limits that had been established during the rules of the early caliphs, Abū Bakr, ʿUmar and ʿAlī, governance became an elitist enterprise closed off to those who did not share a specific tribal allegiance and hierarchy. The saving grace of Muslim governance during its dynastic phase, and one that unfortunately confuses commentators into believing there was good governance, was its administration abilities. Combined with government arms-length relationship with its subjects, this led to the flourishing of many industries and most notably the humanities.

Administrative capacity, however, is only one aspect of governance, the other more critical dimension is the relationship between authorities and subjects or in modern parlance between the state and its citizens. It is through this relationship that publics engage in civic activities, policy problems are defined and designed, resources allocated and long term strategies devised.

Genuine Islamic governance nurtures the relationship between governing authorities and their publics through a process of continuous renewal. Muslims are not subject to human authority by virtue of any absolute rule or divine representation but rather by their own approval based on moral imperative and expressed through a collectively agreed political process. The historic neglect of this relationship or else its characterization as optional contributed to a politically immature community. In light of this deep rooted historical dissonance, the ideas of great political thinkers like Rifāʿah Rāfiʿ al-Ṭahṭāwī (1801-1871), Khayr al-Dīn al-Tūnsī (1820-1890), Jamāl al-Dīn al-Afghānī (1839-1897), Muhammad Abduh (1849-1905), Ahmed Lutfi al-Sayyed (1872-1963), Muhammad al-Ghazali (1917-1996) and Rashid Rida (1865-1935) among others came too late. My aim is not to discuss the differences in their approaches but to highlight that they all recognized the importance of the relationship between the rulers and the ruled, the active participation of citizenry in public affairs, the significant damage that despotism had wreaked on Muslim publics and, in the opinion of a minority, the right of the public to change unjust and oppressive rulers.[69] Al-Sayyed succinctly stated that "the *real* political problem... was the absence of a moral relationship between rulers and ruled."[70]

Thus, Muslims found themselves unprepared when the international shift from governance through dynastic rule to governance through the nation-state transpired. By not establishing and evolving the processes and institutions that had embedded concepts of human rights and civic engagement in the very early days of Islam, Muslim populations became highly vulnerable to foreign invasion, occupation and colonial rule. The emergence of individuals and groups which had not had a chance at leadership during Islam's dynastic reign could now have their turn at power. The lack of practical experience combined with a dearth of scholarship on what the Shariʿah actually contained, facilitated transition from one group of tyrannical rulers to the next. Paradoxically, for many Muslims around the world, it is only through emigration to the west that they have come to experience many of the conditions of governance elaborated in the Shariʿah.

The emergence of a class of Muslim political thinkers and activists with various Islamic ideologies in the 19th and 20th Centuries did not address these deeply disturbing social transformations. Dubbed political Islam, its arrival on the scene actually reinforced some of the very social trends that had subjugated Muslims throughout the centuries. But it did more than this. The Islamic 'awakening' during the colonial period was reactionary and indeed should have emerged much earlier in response to increasingly despondent Muslim rule.

The colonial trigger served to misguidedly position Islam against the 'west' by summing entire populations, albeit mostly non-Muslim, as a foreign other at best and an enemy at worst. Although understandable from a social and political perspective, characterizing Islam as such betrayed the fundamental tenet that Divine law is universal and cannot be appropriated by any side of a conflict. It was mistaken to posit Muslims or Islam against the 'west'; a religion against a geographic location where Islam was present if not in leadership then certainly among local populations. This short-sightedness came to be reflected in the emphasis that political Islam placed on the three key concepts of caliphate, ummah and jihad though a fourth, *shūrā*, is often added for legitimacy and convention as opposed to actual practice. The first would inevitably predispose Islamic politics to authoritarianism.[71]

Generally, the four concepts were uncritically understood within the confines of history as opposed to the expanse of the Shariʿah making political Islam unresponsive to contemporary realities. The incessant emphasis on a caliphate demonstrated a lack of understanding for the institution beyond Islam's very early history including its very clear contemporary inconsistency with *shūrā* and human rights. Similarly, jihad came to be almost exclusively characterized as armed struggle when in actual fact its highest expression was a *word* of truth to a tyrannical ruler,[72] as demonstrated in the traditions of the Prophet and the narratives of the Qur'an. Certainly, the rejection of dynastic rule that had concentrated wealth and power among certain Arab tribes without commensurate involvement of subject populations in matters of governance and policy ought to have been the legitimate focus of jihad. As noted, the concern with who was ruling and how they were ruling appears to have come a little too late.

In light of this, political Islam's actual role in social, political and economic development has been confused and geographically limited. Political Islam has been incapable of addressing the real issues that have subjugated massive numbers of people in the Muslim world. Its preoccupation with outdated modes of governance, lack of viable economic and environmental alternatives, inconsistent record on human rights and poor appreciation of changing global dynamics all spelled failure when the historical moment for its emergence finally appeared on the horizon.

Indeed, it has been over six years since the spark that ignited protests across the Arab world. Beginning in Tunisia on December 18, 2010 and quickly spreading to Egypt, Libya and Yemen dictators were ousted from power from one country after the other. Civil uprisings were quelled in Bahrain and throughout the Arab world while a bloody war continues to ensue in Syria. The former group of countries initially gave the false impression that regime changes were underway and democracy would miraculously follow without institutional or cultural histories, international support and, more serious, without radical transformations of entrenched economic and military interests and deeply embedded corruption. In countries where heads-of-state were ousted, people witnessed the immediate mobilization of military leaderships as well as the transformation of elements of their respective Islamist movements into major political parties.

Even when the Islamist parties who came to the fore had skilled leadership, they lacked the international support, strength, speed and policy acumen to deal with internal challenges that emanated from the military, judiciary, police, security apparatus and otherwise corrupt bureaucracies. They also lacked the ideas, understandings, theories and methodologies that were seriously needed to unify the diverse aspirations of their respective citizenry. What became quickly evident to keen observers was the widespread disagreement over the desired outcomes of the protests and the lack of preparedness of Islamist parties to deal with such complexities. In essence, they had spent decades of social activism among local communities dealing with the *converted* and largely needy social classes who were in no position to make political demands or offer intellectual criticism, while co-opting the very same systems that were reinforcing repression and despotism.

Islamist parties had not foreseen the possibility that Arab citizenry, of all religious suasions, were aspiring toward more open, merciful and just governance systems that respected human rights and freedoms. This significant constituency had envisioned a world more closely integrated with and benefiting from global economics and trade as well as cultural openness, with Islam as a religion presenting a personal moral value system and only then for believers. This miscalculation or political naïveté would see significant numbers of former protesters support the explicit reinstatement of military rule.

Although one cannot credibly argue that a robust Islamic theory of governance and framework for public policies would have altered the course of history, it is important to recognize that the dearth of these elements meant that Islamist parties do not have the tools necessary to carry the publics with them neither domestically nor internationally. Moreover, the publics themselves are scarcely aware of what Islamic governance implies. The explicit or implied recourse to a strict code of corporal punishments, misnamed Shariʿah *law,* in domestic and personal affairs that forebode even greater hardship than in the pre-revolution era alarmed the diverse publics of the Arab world and continues to alarm wider populations both Muslim and non-Muslim elsewhere. In fact, many watched in horror as Islamist parties came to power and rejoiced at their departure.

Explicitly religious or not, state authorities have traditionally been buoyed by important segments within the religious establishment. Even before the downfall of Islamist politics, many prominent scholars, jurists and even Islamist activists had begun realigning themselves with corrupt political powers. Those who were forced to take refuge in other countries on account of their positions during the revolutions, became vocal supporters of the regimes that gave them sanctuary. While understandable, such political about-facing once more neglects Islam's focus on values and principles as opposed to blanket endorsements of political systems, personalities or parties.

Authority of the Religious Establishment

Perhaps the greatest culpability for the state of the Muslim Ummah today lies with the traditional religious establishment. As the self-appointed guardians of the Shariʿah, traditional scholars have taken it upon themselves to correct and preserve "human beings' religion since, if this is denied them, they will suffer the most manifest loss, whereupon none of the blessings they have enjoyed in this world will be of any benefit to them; similarly, their aim is to preserve whatever worldly conditions are essential for [sound] religion to exist and thrive."[73] Unfortunately, a cursory consideration of the state of Muslim affairs amply demonstrates that they have not been up to this task.

Although Islam has no power locus commensurate with the Vatican in Roman Catholicism, jurists and scholars have ensured that the establishment reproduces itself as a powerful, patriarchal, centralized, top-down and predetermined structure operating with strictly defined roles and responsibilities with minor accommodations for changing technologies, values, economics, politics and society. It reserves for itself the articulation of the definition of the Shariʿah, the criteria for the jurist and scholar, the accreditation of places of higher learning, and everyday permissions and prohibitions for believers.[74] Traditional Islamic institutions including universities, national and international fatwa councils and Muslim associations revolve in a universe of their own that does not give adequate voice to other experts, women and youth. Nor does it appear to appreciate the breadth of the Shariʿah and the speed and nature of changing real world contexts.

The artificially constructed limits that traditional jurists have imposed on the Shariʿah through their perceptions of what constitutes jurisprudence (fiqh) and the fundamentals of jurisprudence (*uṣūl* al-fiqh) ought to have limited the relevance of their productions to contemporary governance issues. It is disconcerting that several juristic schools disagree as to the legitimacy of prioritizing human interests over what they perceive to be more directly and explicitly revealed rulings in the scripts. With regards to policy and governance, the jurists have taken one of two major positions. In the first instance they have asserted that the Shariʿah has nothing to say on these matters. In other words, it does not directly or clearly mandate any criteria in these fields.

Any rulings or pronouncements must therefore be classified under what they termed *unrestricted interests* "which are recognized by Islamic Law but which are not mentioned by name in any of the particular legal texts."[75] This concept is used to compensate for the limits of analogical reasoning.[76] Productions related to the *maqāṣid* or the objectives of the Shariʿah as well as Shariʿah-oriented policy or *siyāsah sharʿīyyah* are justified in this way. The second approach has been through the imposition of a never ending process of analogical reasoning akin to the concept of *ever-greening*. In this process, jurists continuously refer to original and often ancient interpretations as opposed to returning to the primary texts for new more relevant understandings.[77] The resulting intractable plethora of isolated, fragmented, and in many cases inconsistent, legal rulings not only obscures important violations of the universals of the Shariʿah but may (un)intentionally have contributed to them as well.

Despite this, the jurists have constructed almost impenetrable boundaries around the exercise of ijtihad, defined by the jurists as independent legal reasoning but more accurately understood as "striving or self-exertion in any activity which entails a measure of hardship."[78] By developing highly formalized and sophisticated rules of ijtihad the enterprise has been effectively closed to experts from other fields and more generally to qualified Muslim thinkers. The scholars of the fundamentals of jurisprudence or *uṣūl al-fiqh* "have laid down certain conditions, such as the qualifications the *mujtahid* must possess, and the set of rules which are designed to ensure the integrity of ijtihad, and to discourage indulgence in arbitrariness or unfounded criticism of others."[79] To guard this system, the establishment endorses a limited number of institutions of higher learning. *Genuine* legal scholars must have attended institutions such as Al Azhar in Egypt, Al Zaytoona in Tunis, Al Qarawiyyin in Morocco, Umm al-Qura in Makkah, Al Hawzat in Iran, and Deoband and Darul-Ulum in India at some point in their legal training.

While there is something to be said for the historical intellectual contributions of these institutions, some of their outstanding graduates and the possibility of evolution toward modern relevance, the prevalence of outdated and politically accommodating curricula that is simply incapable of responding to the challenges of modernity is not reflected in the continued popularity of these centers of learning. In agreement with al-Kawakibi (1848-1902) the "burden of advancing the ethical literacy of society [lay] squarely on the shoulders of the intellectuals in order to combat despotism. He disdained those Muslim intellectuals who placed their mastery of language in the service of political sycophancy or focused their energies on the perfection of dogma and matters related to the afterlife while ignoring he material conditions of ordinary people in this world."[80] I have often observed how aspiring scholars who flock to these institutions from around the world struggle to suspend their critical faculties and disbelief at the conditions prevalent in the societies that house these institutions. Only the recent turmoil in the Middle East may have impacted the influx of students though that is based on safety concerns as opposed to any critical view of the actual output of these institutions or their role in the deterioration of the societies in which they exist. This is particularly anomalous when one considers the relative success of some of the countries from which foreign students originate and the palpable concern that home authorities have with the importation of *foreign* ideas and narrow worldviews. Singapore, for instance, has a re-orientation program for students upon their return from religious studies abroad.

According to Roald the separation of political life from personal religiosity led to a critical deficit in the development of Islamic political ideas while the traditional focus on the private individual, matters of worship and the concerns of micro society gives jurists an almost comprehensive hold on believers. [81] Indeed, the uncritical acceptance of a lack of concern with collective or social issues is due to the historical assertion that if the individual is pious then society will be as well.[82] It follows that if the individual is subservient then stability will be achieved, which is based on a *juristic* preference to avoid conflict.[83] This is a very myopic and short sighted approach to governance and indeed neglects the dynamics of social life as well as the complexities of authority and policy and more notably the relevant processes and substances outlined in the Qur'an.

Yet despite major gaps in their training, Muslim jurists continue to be called upon for policy advice in much the same way that the priesthood was called upon during the Middle Ages in Europe. In the Muslim world, this advice has historically yielded to sectarian rivalries.[84] It is also not uncommon to see scholars giving blanket endorsements and unconditional support to governments that support their causes irrespective of potentially blatant violations of the human rights of those not necessarily aligned with them.

Another problem with the lack of expertise is the likely probability that jurists, whether working as individuals or in groups, will be *captured* by specific interests. Because of their lack of specialized knowledge in other fields, jurists are more prone to adopt positions in response to political pressures. In receiving certain advice from experts, Islamic scholars are no less prone to political manipulation than other professionals and groups. A number of widespread contemporary opinions in areas as diverse as organ donation to genetically modified crops to banking and finance demonstrate how Islamic scholars have buckled under political pressure buoyed by a lack of specialized knowledge and time. As political actors reach out to jurists to support largely predetermined policy agendas the option to provide potentially contradictory opinions or even to insist on the continued search for better and more suitable alternatives rarely appears to be an option. In the fields of governance and public policy this predicament is highly troublesome.

Ironically, experts from other disciplines are often considered as 'intellectuals' but their knowledge, methods and expertise are subordinated to that of the jurist. The jurists may resort to the advice of these experts but in the final analysis recognition of other opinions remains optional. Ramadan argues, "this implicit hierarchy – that is yet so explicit in effect – has the two fold function of clearly defining where 'Islamic authority' should reside and, consequently, who can legitimately state opinions and express themselves in the fields of law and ethics."[85]

Such discrimination is compounded in the perception and engagement of female jurists and scholars. Despite a long and illustrious early history, today's female scholars are marginalized and largely ignored. Most if not all major religious bodies have no female representation, and when they do, it is largely a token gesture. It is also rare to find male scholars citing the works and contributions of their female counterparts from the past or the present. The available volumes which outline such contributions are hardly known and rarely taught in educational curricula.[86] This unacceptable attitude has had profound effects on the status of women in Islam and their regard as notable scholars in Muslim history and among today's Muslims. As a result, an entire perspective is absent from the writings and pronouncement of the traditional religious establishment.

The common, yet unqualified transgressions by jurists into fields of inquiry beyond their narrow legal training, have had serious consequences for Muslims all over the world. A most notable injustice has been the longstanding juxtaposition of national security against the respect and advancement of civil and human rights. The allowance of human rights violations in the name of national stability and defense that is not only aimed at foreign aggressors but increasingly at citizens of the state is a grave error on the part of the jurists. Over time, the compounded effects of state violations toward domestic populations have rendered security threats a smokescreen for despotism and corruption. It is difficult to accept that this has gone unnoticed by the religious establishment. According to the late Mahmood Ghazi, "Justice is at the core of the Shariʿah, but because it was perhaps difficult for the Islamic scholars to tell these leaders to focus on these areas, they didn't do it."[87] Within this dynamic, however, the average believer is also blameworthy.

Authority of the Muslim Mind

Centuries of indoctrination, juridification[88] and usurpation have impacted the Muslim mind's willingness and capacity to reason about matters of faith including the ability to construct, verify and reform the content of its beliefs. Al-Alwani asserts that "one of the most salient manifestations of the crisis of the Muslim mind is an imbalance in the standards and priorities on the basis of which it has come to operate."[89] The hegemony of traditional jurisprudence with its strict rules of ijtihad combined with linguistic illiteracy of both Arab and non-Arab natives has forced individuals and communities to rely almost exclusively on their religious leaders and local imams or even on distant imams via social media. This does not permit believers to "actualize norms of autonomy that are located within self, community and society."[90] Diverse Muslim populations have very limited choices in terms of source references and Islamic expertise especially in their language and from their cultural perspectives.

It is not surprising that knowledge of what Islamic policy and governance entail is very limited. Moosa suggests that "the real damage of decades of authoritarianism has been the denial of people's opportunity to think and actualize the ethical teachings of their religions."[91] Public opinion varies widely depending on a community's religious and political leadership, media, understandings acquired over one's life course and local contexts. Conceptions of Islam in the public sphere range from no role to coercive community practices, and in particular, the imposition of a strict penal code and corporal punishments. The only common thread between these extreme poles is a lack of understanding of what genuine Islamic governance actually means. It is common to find culturally diverse populations trying to address dissimilar problems by adapting the same Islamic rulings that are not only ancient but ill-suited for the task. Often times the scholars and literature resorted to are not equipped to respond to public challenges but the will, ability and confidence to return to the primary sources is lacking.

Muslims continue to rely on local religious leaders or well-known foreign scholars via social media to solicit opinions on a range of issues from the most mundane to more serious matters. In doing so, they betray a clear command in the Qur'an not to ask too many questions. God has cautioned believers against such practice for a number of reasons. The most profound justification being to maintain the widest possible scope for human inquiry and creativity without rigidity or sacred obligation. This permits an emergence and respect for a diversity of equally valid alternatives to an infinite number of human preferences. "Oh you who believe, do not ask questions about things if made plain to you would cause you hardship. But if you ask about things as the Qur'an is being revealed they will be made plain to you. God will pardon those [questions], for He is oft forgiving, most forbearing" (5:181). Believers are urged to resort to their *fiṭrah* or innate nature as well as all the information and knowledge that are available to them for the formulation of appropriate positions. As Rashid Rida had observed:

> The essence of the universality of Islam and the mission of Prophet Muhammad, God's peace and blessings be upon him, does not become evident until we live and establish Islam on the basis of rationalism... Those who oppose this rational free-thinking approach put themselves in opposition to God and completely undermine the essence of the Shariʿah of Islam and its relevance and effect. Through their ignorance they do a great disservice to Islam.[92]

The requirement that Muslims actively contribute to the advancement of human welfare in its complex modern forms demands leading, deep and confident thought in every field of human endeavor. Believers are warned against being passive followers or unsuspecting leaders. Every person will be called to account for his or her choices on the Day of Judgment. The Qur'an states: "And do not follow that of which you have no knowledge for the hearing, the sight and the heart are all accountable" (*al-Isrā'*: 36). The hyper trend of incessantly consulting religious leaders on every affair as opposed to self-reflection or collective decision-making has dampened religious knowledge and defeated gradual progress towards more democratic processes of governance. One must also draw attention to the distracting and socially distorting effects of Islam as a form entertainment and its scholars and preachers as "stars", both of which defy Islamic morality and ethics.

Fortunately, a good number of Muslims continue to be concerned with the nature and role of Divine rights in their lives, while the Qur'an and Sunnah continue to play a central role in their day-to-day activities. A growing constituency of marginalized groups including men, women, youth, and scholars from within the tradition as well as other disciplines and traditions are increasingly questioning passive obedience to narrow legal authority that has largely divorced itself from the realities and needs faced by Muslims and non-Muslims today. These individuals and communities have grown impatient with the religious establishment's restrictive legal edicts while neglecting human rights, and especially those of women, and other important public concerns. They recognize the limited applicability of traditional jurisprudence to their daily struggle and longer term aspirations. Around the world, believers are seeking knowledge and approaches that can not only help them remain faithful to Islam but that will enable them to use their faith to improve their lives and the lives of those around them. There is a growing constituency of individuals, groups, organizations and governments, Muslim and non-Muslim, looking for effective ways to deal with contemporary challenges and who, most importantly, are open to acknowledging a Divine reference.

Conclusion

This chapter has argued that the relationship of Muslims to authority is characterized by rule through three proxies including the state, the traditional religious establishment and the Muslim mind. In particular, it proposed that the dynamics between the state and Islamic scholars over the centuries, and more recently, the Islamic political movement has played an important role in subjugating Muslim publics. Although the picture is infinitely more complex than discussed above, it is safe to say that none of these actors have been genuinely interested in establishing systems of governance for the people based on the people's aspirations and needs as well as on critical global imperatives. Early scholars became implicated in supporting state repression by misguidedly condoning domestic injustice if not directly through formal pronouncements then indirectly by not giving believing publics the justifications and tools to fight despotism. Not surprisingly the introduction of political Islam did not fare much better. Without a robust theory of governance, an open attitude toward pluralism and public participation, and an uncompromising stand against corruption and injustice, political Islam served to reinforce the very structures it sought to challenge. The challenge of politics presents two confounding realities. On the one hand, are the deeply entrenched though diverse, authoritarian dictatorships throughout the Muslim world. Even in instances where there appears to be some semblance of democracy, the state's tight hold on authority and tendencies toward dictatorship do not bode well for genuine advancement and pluralism. On the other hand, the Islamist movement appears to have reinforced this situation by missing a critical historical moment to present something preferable to both Muslim and non-Muslim publics. The movement's general inability to detect the pulse of the public during the recent wave of protests across the Arab world combined with a dearth of policy alternatives that were direly needed to address acute economic crises and check corrupt military establishments, demonstrated political immaturity and doctrinal ignorance. Today, the movement is in a fragmented mess with major internal divisions and a lack of direction. Many of its leadership and youth have been vilified and incarcerated in a political bid to eliminate the movement altogether. This predicament was no doubt exacerbated by the direct and indirect role of Muslim jurists and scholars, who represent the second authoritative proxy for Muslims. Their historical role in the political arena has been complex, confused and divisive, with at least a notable segment ready and willing to change sides as political fortunes dictate.

Others appear to reject nationalist loyalties toward the state of their citizenship but inevitably align themselves with other state governments that serve their interests or what they perceive to be the interests of the Islamic movement. This is undertaken both individually and as part of more organized bodies potentially pitting governments and believers against one another. In the private sphere scholars have been no less divisive, each rejoicing with a historically developed identity that betrays the unity of Islam's original message. The erection of high intellectual barriers to ijtihad reinforces an elitist approach that has usurped the religious independence of common folk, who have generally relinquished responsibility to understand and interpret Islam given the perceived gravity of independent undertakings. Even as sizable numbers of Muslims attain expertise in diverse fields of knowledge around the world this reluctance continues, which brings us to the third major challenge highlighted in this chapter, the Muslim mind. It would appear that centuries of indoctrination and usurpation have rendered the Muslim mind unwilling and many cases incapable of independently verifying and reforming the content of its beliefs. This endeavor becomes even more contentious when presented with the possibility of public debate and scrutiny. Paradoxically, this complacency goes against the teachings in the Qur'an and Sunnah.

Those who appreciate the need for reform and reinterpretation as well as the need to explore the Shariʿah for its wisdom on diverse human affairs, face unprecedented difficulty due to the lack of alternative approaches. Credible alternatives based on the primary Islamic sources need to be developed and nurtured to give support and credence to these efforts. Creative Islamic thinkers often find themselves marginalized by mainstream coreligionists or discounted by secular counterparts. Indeed, the quest for genuine Islamic governance and public policy for and by Muslims as expounded throughout this book requires a three-pronged approach that aims to liberate people from the tyranny of political authorities, the hegemony of traditional legal scholars and jurists, and above all from their own reluctance, lack of self-confidence, or else self-inflicted ignorance of the spirit of the Shariʿah.

II
Public Policy in Islam: The State of the Discipline

3

The Historical Roots of *Maqāṣid* Studies

> Every legal ruling in Islam has a function which it performs, an aim which it realizes, a cause, be it explicit or implicit, and an intention which it seeks to fulfill and all of this in order to realize benefit to human beings or to ward off harm or corruption.
>
> TAHA JABIR ALALWANI[93]

This chapter introduces the *maqāṣid* approach to Islamic studies. My aim is to show an appreciation for this intellectual contribution while at the same time highlighting important critiques that ought to be considered by contemporary *maqāṣid* scholars who aspire to extend this approach to policy and governance. The study of *maqāṣid* has grown out of the works of tenth century scholars who sought to remedy the gaps between Islamic jurisprudence and Muslim practice and what they perceived to be the higher goals of the Shariʿah. The *maqāṣid* approach is primarily credited to the work of Imam Abū Isḥāq al-Shāṭibī, writing in the fourteenth century and most distinguishably articulated in his *al-Muwāfaqāt fī Uṣūl al-Sharīʿah* (Correspondences in the Fundamentals of Revealed Law) in which he advanced the *maqāṣid* approach in a number of unprecedented ways.[94] Al-Raysuni, who undertook a seminal and detailed study titled *Imam al-Shāṭibī's Theory of the Higher Objectives and Intents of Islamic Law*, observed:

> Indeed, who could fittingly undertake a study of the objectives of Islamic Law without also undertaking an in-depth study of the objectives which were dear to al-Shāṭibī's own heart? For if truth be told, research into the objectives of Islamic Law has, to this day, still not matched, much less surpassed, what al-Shāṭibī achieved in this sphere.[95]

Al-Shāṭibī among other notable jurists that preceded him, articulated a critical understanding of the need to overlay fiqh with the objectives of the Shariʿah, or what had come to be known as *maqāṣid-al-sharīʿah*, which was dedicated to the rigorous application of the purposes or objectives of the Shariʿah to religion, basic rules and universal belief.[96] Collectively, the works of early *maqāṣid* scholars aimed to re-orient fiqh toward greater justice, mercy, wisdom and welfare. Ibn al-Qayyim (d.1350) succinctly states:

> Verily, the Sharia is founded upon wisdom and welfare for worshipers in this life and the afterlife. In its entirety it is justice, mercy, benefit, and wisdom. Every matter which abandons justice for tyranny, mercy for cruelty, benefit for corruption, and wisdom for foolishness is not a part of the Sharia even if it was introduced therein by an interpretation.[97]

These early scholars clearly recognized the need to improve the practice and study of jurisprudence through the introduction of a comprehensive ethical framework. Their work reflected a growing disenchantment with the legal artifices with which many jurists had become obsessed at the expense of honoring the objectives of the law. For al-Juwaynī (d.1085), "whoever fails to comprehend the objectives which underlie the [Divine] commands and prohibitions has likewise failed to perceive the basis for the establishment of the Law."[98]

In light of this, the chapter is divided into three main parts. In the first part, I present a perspective on history that helps shed light on modern governance and policy dilemmas in Muslim communities. The suggestion that the history of *Islamic* governance is characterized by a 'Shariʿah paradigm' or a glorious past that was unfortunately interrupted by western domination is not acceptable and does not conform with what we know of Divine law. The Qur'an tells us: "...God does not change the bounty with which He has graced a nation, until they have changed what is in their own selves, He is the Hearer the Knower" (*al-Anfāl*: 53). The second part, therefore, presents the contribution of some of the most renowned Islamic jurists and scholars in our history. These jurists understood the destructive changes that had taken place not only in governance but also among their contemporaries. The *maqāṣid* approach can be considered the intellectual response that they presented in an attempt to re-orient Islamic legal thought. Finally, in the third part of the chapter I offer an account of the evolution of the classical *maqāṣid* approach as developed by contemporary scholars.

A Perspective on History

Though formal study of *maqāṣid* commenced in the tenth century or a bit earlier, the concept had been appreciated and practiced prior to Arabia's relapse into tribal bigotry and subsequent rule by authoritarian dynasties. Interestingly, the use of *maqāṣid* was most evident in governance and policy when the early caliphs realized that they had to draw on an approach that enabled enough flexibility to govern while remaining true to the objectives of their newly embraced religion. There is, however, a clear distinction between the practice of *maqāṣid* by early rulers like Abū Bakr, ʿUmar and ʿAlī, and the *maqāṣid* approach as it came to be detailed, studied and disseminated by later jurists. The relative lack of freedom, power and holistic knowledge of the latter did not see the *maqāṣid* approach regain the prominence that it had enjoyed during the reign of the early caliphs.

The early practice of *maqāṣid* was distinguishable from the articulations of later jurists in three important ways:

1. The early application of the *maqāṣid* approach was explicitly problem and context oriented. The combination of knowledge, power and piety endued the early caliphs with the spiritual and material convictions to pursue the essence of Islam thereby rejecting literal readings of the text when this betrayed its perceived objectives given actual circumstances. All of the Companions (of the Prophet) generally applied "their own sense of public interest (*maṣlaḥah*) especially those who were in government positions."[99]
2. This meant that in its original expression, the *maqāṣid* approach was not bound by the strict fundamentals of jurisprudence or any other intellectual boundary. The early caliphs' unrivalled understanding of fiqh which accepted an intrinsic and organic element of purposefulness allowed for the broad incorporation of all areas of knowledge when addressing policy challenges. They did this while vehemently protecting the fundamental tenets of the faith.

3. In the sphere of governance, these tenets included an unwavering commitment to *shūrā* or collective decision-making and an uncompromising stand for human dignity (*karāmah*). Abū Bakr's early days saw the waging of war against those who wished to retract payment of *zakat*, which the central authority was using to support social welfare, among other programs, for the poor. ʿUmar is perhaps best known for his renowned anti-slavery statement: "On what grounds do you enslave people whose mothers have born them free?"[100] Undoubtedly, this emphasis on values highlighted the inescapable application of the higher purposes of Islam in policy and governance.

With the rise of authoritarian dynasties after the rule of ʿAlī ibn Abī Ṭālib, the *maqāṣid* approach would only occasionally be perceptible during Islam's long dynastic reign. While the new rulers innovated widely in policy and administration,[101] the link to *shūrā* and fiqh as understood and practiced by the early caliphs ceased.[102] Dynastic rule may have resulted in a separation of law and 'state', as Hallaq argues,[103] but it did so at the expense of the unity that was evident in the early Islamic governance model which exhibited greater democratic tendencies. If government, as Hallaq further claims, was only exceptionally intervening in law and society, it was not due to any respect of boundaries but rather a tacit agreement that the latter, would in return, not make pronouncements on governance and the alternation of political power.

The growing role of jurists and judges in running civic affairs[104] served to mask their religious and intellectual confinement. The law became limited to regulating the economic and social affairs of subjects, while the distinction between fiqh (or the jurists' understandings) and the Shariʿah (or unchanging and all-encompassing Divine law) became increasingly blurred. Civilian populations were subject to the law of the jurists, while public servants were subject to the laws of the ruler neither of which had the right to claim divinity. The sultan was only ceremoniously subject to religious law. To characterize the resulting system of governance as Islamic is simply not accurate.[105]

The actual result was a system of governance increasingly alienated from its subjects, who were not only incapable of ascertaining their rights vis-à-vis their rulers but who were additionally betrayed by a religious establishment that had been entrusted with their care. Aḥmad ibn Taymiyyah (d. 1328) for instance, who actively criticized the social and political ills of his time, also condoned government repression and misconduct in the name of protecting the ummah from foreign aggression. Impacted by the Mongol invasions, Ibn Taymiyyah subordinated objectives such as freedom, participation, consultation and social justice to measures that allegedly protected the *state*.[106] Ibn Taymiyyah himself would die in a Damascus prison at age sixty-five on account of his radical views.[107] But to say that the jurists objected to and sometime militated against such policies as "legalizing usury, extra judicial taxes, and torture..."[108] does not absolve them from responsibility. A responsibility that ought to have entailed empowering the subjects of the *state* to demand the reinstatement of their divinely ordained dignity even if through rebellion.

Policies and administrative measures that were not objectionable to the jurists were classified as *siyāsah sharᶜiyyah* or Shariᶜah-based politics, which relies on the juristic construct of unrestricted interests or *al-maṣāliḥ al-mursalah*. These "were mostly seen and accepted as an integral part of the legal culture and as an extrajudicial element that was required – after all – by the siyasa shar'eyyah itself."[109] The insinuation that policy and governance were beyond the realm of fiqh and as such not directly or clearly addressed in the Shariᶜah created a double conundrum. First, and most serious, it divided the Shariᶜah in a way that was not religiously possible, elevating and prioritizing some 'legal' elements while devaluing and dismissing others. This partial, fragmented and micro approach to the Shariᶜah was not conducive to the law, let alone to matters of policy and governance. Second, it gave the impression of an unrestricted expanse for government action where the Shariᶜah's actual holistic, cumulative and integrative nature had no say. The idea of the *maqāṣid* appears to have been lost on both the jurists and the rulers, while the subjects of authority became accustomed to yielding to the dictates of both.

Dynastic rule spelled the end of good governance including leadership based on merit and public approval.[110] Arab tribes persecuted each other. Dynasties held on to power as long as they could by suppressing opposition and maintaining strong enough alliances to keep enemies at bay.[111] According to Syed:

> The more thoughtful and religious-minded people now withdrew from all interest in public affairs; they devoted themselves to the cultivation of literature, to the pursuit of Islamic jurisprudence, – the first foundations which were laid at this period, – or to the quiet observance of the rules of their religion. They helped in the propagation of the Faith, but took no part in the government of the Empire.[112]

It was during this time that a group of renowned jurists began to revive the concept of *maqāṣid*. Their efforts were aimed at exhorting their contemporaries to heed the objectives of the Shariʿah in making legal pronouncements and interpreting the texts.

Development of the *Maqāṣid* Approach

There is broad agreement regarding the origins and development of the *maqāṣid* as an idea and later as a philosophy of Islamic law among a broad spectrum of contemporary scholars of Islamic jurisprudence. The following highlights several of the major contributions that early scholars made to the development of the *maqāṣid* approach. The presentation of these contributions can be found in greater detail in the works of others who specialize in *maqāṣid* studies. The discussion here is intended to reinforce the legitimacy of the approach through its historical grounding and elaboration by several distinguished jurists, whose broad influence in fiqh continues to this day.

Abū al-Maʿālī al-Juwaynī (d. 1085) suggested that Islamic law was intended to protect the faith, souls, minds, private parts, and the money of people. Collectively, these objectives or *maqāṣid* were considered the *essentials* of Islamic jurisprudence commonly conflated with the Shariʿah. The essentials were perceived as the positive corollaries of the rulings that had to do with the laws of retribution and, as such, the interests without which life cannot proceed. Based on al-Juwaynī's proposition, early scholars classified the *maqāṣid* as essentials (*ḍarūriyyāt*), needs (*ḥajiyāt*) or embellishments (*taḥsīniyyāt*) based on their urgency and clarity. Needs are less essential for human life, and embellishments as the concept suggests, are add-ons or "beatifying purposes"[113] or "refinements of peoples customs and conduct."[114] Needs and embellishments are considered to serve and protect the levels above them. However, should an interest initially classified as a need or embellishment become negatively affected and extensively deficient it may be escalated to a higher level to emphasize the urgency of addressing its loss.

Attention was drawn to the specific order of the *maqāṣid* by one of al-Juwaynī's students. Abū Ḥamīd al-Ghazālī (d. 1111) prioritized the objectives in the following order: faith, soul, mind, offspring and wealth. He also introduced the idea that the Shariʿah sought to *preserve* these essentials through its various rulings. From henceforth *maqāṣid* scholars would refer to the preservation of the various essentials or necessities.

As Islamic scholars continued to elaborate the *maqāṣid* approach and develop its underlying philosophy, it became important to link what they perceived as the objectives of the Shariʿah with human interests (*maṣāliḥ*). This was the major contribution of al-ʿIzz ibn ʿAbd al-Salām (d. 1209) who placed a spotlight on the link between any juridical ruling and its purpose. In fact, he went so far as to suggest that "every action that misses its purpose is void."[115]

The sixth *maqṣad* would be introduced by Shihāb al-Dīn al-Qarāfī (d. 1285). Al-Qarāfī reasoned that if the basis of the other objectives were the rulings associated with corporal punishments, then the preservation of honour needed to be added. The preservation of honour, claimed al-Qarāfī was the positive corollary of the punishment for slander or the bearing of false witness. Al-Qarāfī also differentiated between the different intents of the Prophet in his different capacities. He asserted that the Prophet's conveyance of the Divine message constituted mandatory injunctions for believers, whereas his pronouncements in other capacities were open to adjustments based on changing contexts. Finally, al-Qarāfī contributed to the idea of facilitating the means that achieve good ends, as a corollary to blocking the means that may lead to harmful ends, which was already broadly accepted.

Shams al-Dīn ibn al-Qayyim (d. 1347) contributed to the *maqāṣid* approach by providing a detailed critique of juridical tricks or *ḥiyal*. A juridical trick occurs when an individual carries out an act that appears lawful on the surface, however, neither the intention nor the objective of act are lawful. Juridical tricks continue to be resorted to in order to avoid what some scholars consider excessive strictness of Islamic law. They are particularly popular in economics and finance where Islam prohibits usurious transactions. In my view, juridical tricks have been instrumental in justifying corrupt practices. Close scrutiny reveals that it is not the strictness of the law that is at issue but rather the poverty of our understanding of the Shariʿah, its objectives and practical applications or else an attempt to avoid what is clearly understood but not desired.

Ibn Taymiyyah (d. 1328) had noted that the *maqāṣid* of his predecessors were derived "from punishments imposed on those who violate them."[116] He thus sought to "open the *Maqāṣid* to wider values, including justice, virtue, constitutional rights, and scientific excellence among others."[117] Many scholars however, refused to include the higher values he enumerated as separate *maqāṣid* insisting that they are intrinsic to the original six objectives.[118] This era of early contributions would close with that of Abū Isḥāq al-Shāṭibī (d. 1388) the most celebrated of all early *maqāṣid* scholars.

It is generally agreed that al-Shāṭibī was the most influential theorist among the early *maqāṣid* scholars. It was he who ascertained how the *maqāṣid* of the Lawgiver could be determined. According to Attia, everyone who came after al-Shāṭibī either summarized or rearranged his work.[119] The three bases for the law that al-Shāṭibī outlined included:

1. Explicit texts from the Qur'an or the Sunnah which identify the basis or occasion (*ʿillah*) of Islamic rulings.
2. Inductive analysis of the actions of the Lawgiver, which may be divided into two types. The first type is an inductive reading of the legal rulings whose bases (*ʿilal*) have been determined by means of recognized approaches (*masālik al-ʿillah*), yet without an explicit text from the Qur'an or the Sunnah. The second is an inductive reading of the various pieces of textual evidence in support of legal

rulings which have a common purpose (*ghāyah*) and basis (*baᶜith*).

3. The Companions' understanding of the rulings in the Qur'an and the Sunnah.[120]

The sources of the rulings from which the *maqāṣid* were thus derived include the primary sources of the Qur'an and Sunnah and the secondary sources of the different schools of jurisprudence which include, i.e., consensus (*ijmāᶜ*), analogy (*qiyās*), interest (*maṣlaḥah*), preference (*istiḥsān*), blocking the means (*sad al-dharā'iᶜ*), presumption of continuity (*al-istiṣḥāb*); as well as normative judgments, i.e., customs (*ᶜurf*), previous jurisprudence (*sharᶜ man qablanā*), and a Companion's opinion (*fatwah ṣaḥābī*).[121] Al-Shāṭibī insisted that applying an inductive approach to these sources in order to derive the *maqāṣid* leads to "complete certainty."[122] Each *maqṣad* is based on multiple evidences that when taken together "convey a single message which is thereby invested with complete certitude."[123]

Although al-Shāṭibī used the same terminology as his predecessors he refined and elevated the approach in a way that those before him had not. Al-Shāṭibī's book *Al-Muwāfaqāt fī Uṣūl al-Sharīᶜah* (Correspondences in the Fundamentals of Revealed Law) would emerge as the standard reference on the *maqāṣid* until the twentieth century.[124] In it he accomplished three important feats: (1) established the *maqāṣid* as fundamentals of Islamic law, i.e., 'fundamentals of religion, basic rules of the law, and universals of belief'; (2) insisted on the supremacy of the *maqāṣid* over its partial rulings, making any ruling that betrayed the *maqāṣid* incorrect; and (3) demonstrated that the process by which the *maqāṣid* were determined was certain, i.e., not open to doubt.[125]

Taken together, the contributions of early scholars drew attention to the importance of understanding and honoring what they deemed to be the higher purposes of Islamic law. Their productions expressed recognition that something in the enterprise had gone wrong and needed fixing if Islamic jurisprudence was to fulfill its intended purpose. Unless the *maqāṣid* were incorporated into the fundamentals of Islamic jurisprudence so that they remained foremost in the mind of the scholar as he formulated his opinions, it was likely that the law would increasingly betray its purpose. Under no circumstances could the building blocks of an edifice that demanded mercy, justice, welfare and wisdom accept less than this.

Contemporary Evolution of the *Maqāṣid* Approach

The *maqāṣid* approach was intended to provide an ethical framework for the law particularly as elaborated in the traditional works of jurisprudence. The major characteristics of the approach, however, make it amenable to application in a wide range of disciplines, and in particular, governance and policy, which are considered its original breeding grounds. The following sections present a closer look at each of the essentials. By tracing their evolution and shift into governance, these sections pay special attention to the contribution of the Shariah Index Project (SIP) which brought together the most outstanding names in the field today.[126]

Preservation of Religion

The objective or *maqṣad* of the preservation of religion (*dīn*), in its original meaning referred to the preservation of Islam, which was considered the positive corollary for the punishment of apostasy. *Dīn* is defined as doctrinal philosophy, rites and rituals. With such a narrow definition it was possible for scholars to justify the evolution of this objective to freedom of religions. The SIP argues that "this *maqṣad* prescribes the promotion of Islamic ethical values, freedom of religious choice, and the facilitation of religious practice to those who have made this choice." Accordingly, it is the "state's duty to encourage and promote the positive with regards to religious practice, rather than to prevent what one religion or religious interpretation deems negative."[127] The scholars are rightly concerned with the state's power to enforce specific religious views on its citizens or to reprimand them for what its authorities deem unacceptable. This challenge emerges because Islam has often been conflated with a particular school of law or *madhhab* and thus a certain interpretation. In essence, the scholars wanted to maintain the freedom of Muslims to practice Islam as they see fit without state interference.

Commensurately, the SIP also emphasizes the principle of religious freedom, which entails the protection of non-Muslim populations in states that are predominantly Muslim. Thus, non-Muslims are permitted to consume alcohol, something that is strictly prohibited in Islam. It also means partial support "for their houses of worship and religious schools, a support that may even be financial."[128] The scholars often refer their positions on freedom of religion to the Qur'anic injunction that "there is no compulsion in religion" (*al-Baqarah*: 256).

While the accommodating spirit that infuses this scholarly approach toward the preservation of religion is appreciated, it lacks the analytic orientation that would be required for robust policy making. The conclusions of the scholars reflect the drive to shape the *maqāṣid* in such a way that would garner the least resistance from Muslims from different sects as well as from non-Muslims. The *maqāṣid*, however, were not intended as an accommodating framework that serves only to bridge diverse opinions or justify the status quo. To add value, the approach must remain capable of presenting society with credible objectives and the means to attaining them rather than expressing ever increasing elasticity.

In light of this, the shift away from the understanding of *dīn* as Islam is problematic and not reflective of Qur'anic teachings. The Qur'an clearly states: "Surely the *Dīn* with God is Islam..." (*Āl ʿImrān*: 19). Reference to *Dīn* as religion, albeit its literal translation, empties the term of its *maqāṣidī* meaning and betrays the values that are inherent to Islam which undoubtedly include freedom of belief and conscience. The preservation of religion in its original exposition does not mean religion narrowly speaking but refers to Islam in its comprehensive understanding. Many contemporary scholars have shifted away from the strict equation of *Dīn* to Islam, and thus, have preferred to use the English term 'religion'. According to Auda "the same theory for that purpose of the Islamic Law has been re-interpreted to mean a dramatically different concept, which is 'freedom of faiths,' to use Ibn Ashur's words, or 'freedom of belief,' in other contemporary expressions."[129]

This is problematic because it divorces Islam from the values that actually comprise its core doctrine. **Freedom of belief is a fundamental right in the Qur'an and Sunnah. It should not constitute an *evolution* of understanding but rather a pillar of Islam's original message.** To state otherwise is to feign the introduction of a new element and have to suffer the possibility of popular rejection.

Obscuring the correspondence of *Dīn* with Islam serves to alienate the *maqāṣid* from an explicit and direct link with Islam. Islam is not a product of the *maqāṣid*, nor is it an equal along with other religions or systems of belief, but rather the *maqāṣid* are a product of Islam while other monotheistic religions are included under Islam's broad umbrella. What needs to be understood is the meaning of *Dīn* as Islam, and thus, what it is to be *Muslim* in the Shariʿah and in turn, what this means for governance.

The *Dīn* in the Qur'an is the religion that God has chosen for believers throughout the ages (*Āl ʿImrān*: 83). In its most fundamental meaning *Dīn* implies submission or *islām* to God's will, that being whatever God has guided his servants toward in expression of their ultimate and unyielding belief in Him, the One True God (*al-Bayyinah*: 5). A comprehensive understanding of *Dīn* includes an Islam that does not necessarily entail the rituals that would later characterize the message of Prophet Muhammad for all of humankind. Actually, the Qur'an stresses that to each people are "appointed rites which they must follow" and that the right to do so is not open to disputation (*al-Ḥajj*: 67). *Al*-Ghazali provides an illustrative metaphor:

> In today's technological terms, the national power grid in certain small towns can extend to only a few square kilometers, whereas in big cities it has to cover hundreds or perhaps thousands of times that area; however, the electric current flowing through both grid systems remains the same and performs the same function.[130]

Thus, prophets Abraham and Jacob both advised their sons that God had chosen their *Dīn* for them and thereby they should not die except as Muslims (*al-Baqarah*: 132). Likewise, Moses advised his people to put their trust in God if they are Muslims (*Yūnus*: 84). And the disciples who pledged to be God's victors also witnessed that they were Muslim (*al-Mā'idah*: 111). By way of confirmation and final evidence God tells us that He named the believers of all ages Muslim (*al-Ḥajj*: 78). The ultimate thread that binds all believers is the essence of this one true *Dīn*.

It is this understanding of *Dīn* around which we are commanded to find common ground. Although to each people is a *shirʿah* or way and means of expression, the ultimate goal is one. The Qur'an thus states: "Say: O People of the Book come to a word that is equal between us and you, that we shall not worship except God and we shall not associate anything with Him and that we will not take from among ourselves lords other than God..." (*Āl ʿImrān*: 64). It further states: "And they [People of the Book] have been commanded nothing other than to worship God, faithful to the religion He has chosen, turning away from all that is false and harmful, and establishing prayer, and giving zakat, and this is the invaluable religion" (*al-Bayyinah*: 5). It is through this concept of *Dīn*, properly understood, that all believers are united irrespective of the diversity of beliefs and expressions.

We live in a world of infinite religious diversity and even of much disbelief and this is something that we have to grapple with especially in the field of governance and policy. There is no compulsion in *Dīn* (*al-Baqarah*: 256). No person or group can be forced to believe, and indeed this is not the role of any governing authority. The Qur'an states: "And say the truth is from your Lord: So who wills may believe, and who wills may disbelieve..." (*al-Kahf*: 29). Every subject or citizen of the state must be guaranteed an equal and adequate level of rights and freedoms including freedom of religion and conscience.

That said, the *maqāṣid* approach to governance clearly entails the preservation of *Dīn* as Islam. The primary concern of *maqāṣid* studies should not be the potential emergence of conflicts, but rather with illuminating the values and objectives that Muslims share with others. A proper understanding of the Shariʿah will help us mitigate potential disagreements without compromising on the true meaning of the *maqāṣid*.

Preservation of Life

The *maqṣad* or objective of the preservation of life (*nafs*) "is evidenced by the law of retribution in the event of murder"[131] and generally has not been subject to much evolution in terminology among contemporary scholars except in the sense of how it is to be achieved. The SIP scholars note that this objective "refers generally to the protection of physical life, provision of basic physical needs, and the prevention of harm to the body."[132] The scholars thus focused on the necessity of national security, the extent of extending of protection to non-citizens, and the preservation of the environment.

As with the concept of *Dīn*, this concept of life or *nafs* does not capture the full meaning alluded to in the Shariʿah. The concept is much richer than the physical manifestation of life. The Qur'an informs us that God created us from a single being or *nafs* (*al-Nisā'*: 1; *al-Aʿrāf*: 189), the same concept used to denote the preservation of life (*ḥifẓ al-nafs*). The concept of *nafs* in the Qur'an connects humanity like no other concept. To preserve the *nafs* presupposes acknowledgement of this fundamental fact. Humanity is bound together by its source and by the primacy of mercy in our relations. Thus, when God decrees upon the Children of Israel that he who kills a *nafs* or corrupts in the earth is as if he killed all people and he who revives a *nafs* is as if he revived all people (5:32), we recognize the extent of our interdependencies. Interdependency is a part of human nature as God created us from *ʿalaq* or a substance that clings or attaches itself (*al-ʿAlaq*: 2). Humanity is intrinsically interdependent.[133] Characterizing humans by their nature of attachment emphasizes our physical, emotional and social needs to identify with others, with interests and with nature. Interdependence is a fundamental feature of all living creatures.

Therefore, life in the absence of social communities is void of meaning and in many cases impossible. Life depends on an intricate web of relations that Islam nurtures and regulates for general welfare. The ultimate accountability of every *nafs* is closely associated with its role, behavior and contribution to these social relations. The Qur'an also exhorts us to be cognizant that all creatures form communities similar to ours so that our regard for social relations is not limited to the human realm. Protecting the environment must include an appreciation of the relationships within and among communities of other living creatures. If we are not to nurture them, then at least we should desist from harming them.

In light of this, the focus on the physical side of life while necessary is certainly not sufficient. There must be serious efforts to ensure that government policy recognizes the necessity of healthy social relations that support life systems. The preservation of *nafs* must respect the concept of life upon which life is dependent, that is, beyond physical existence.

Measures that support human security, social inclusion and community bonds are some areas where policy can play a positive role. Moreover, this Qur'anic concept of *nafs* points to the necessity of enabling a robust civil society, voluntarism and charitable activities. More technical areas include immigration and refugee policies that might encourage family reunifications. They also include environmental policies that re-envision the rights of creation. These are very complex issues. The point to be made here is that the preservation of life is certainly not limited to a physical phenomenon but rather to the protection and advancement of communities and societies as mutually interdependent systems.

Preservation of the Mind

The preservation of the mind (*ᶜaql*) originally sprang from the prohibition against intoxicants. According to Auda it is "currently evolving to include 'propagation of scientific thinking,' 'travelling to seek knowledge,' 'suppressing the herd mentality,' and 'avoiding brain drain.'"[134] The SIP scholars appear to echo these developments.[135] They emphasize that education is a duty for every Muslim, male and female. Governments should provide for quality secular and spiritual education for all its citizens. They should also promote innovation and invest in science and technology, which necessitates freedom of speech and expression. This discussion does not preclude the state's role in prohibiting intoxicants for Muslims, however, the balance of efforts should be related to persuasion and exposing the harms of consumption as opposed to simple prohibition.[136]

There is no doubt that literacy and education are at the heart of Islam – a religion that commenced with an injunction to read in the name of the Lord that created (*al-ᶜAlaq*: 1). This is an immediate connection between the written (recited) word and the experienced (discovered) word. The Shariᶜah harmonizes an infinite diversity of elements in a holistic purposeful system that serves the needs of all mutually interdependent beings. Ramadan spends considerable and commendable effort insisting that the sources of *uṣūl al-fiqh* (the fundamentals of jurisprudence) must encompass the social and natural sciences as well as our continuously expanding knowledge of the universe.[137] He argues, "any coherent thought... aiming at reforming today's world must devise a dynamic *fiqh*, taking into account the time factor, intellectual and social dynamics, and dialectic tensions between higher objectives, universal principles, and historical models: such a *fiqh* should certainly not rigidify normative categories for fear of scientific, social, and human complexities that elude it."[138] What Ramadan draws attention to in our context is that preservation of the mind has to start with Islamic jurisprudence itself, including the way in which we have derived and explained the *maqāṣid*. Policy and governance are multi-disciplinary, multi-method, problem oriented and context specific fields that will necessarily demand a much wider, deeper and complex command of the Shariᶜah.

Undoubtedly, the preservation of the Arabic language is a critical concern. The Qur'an was revealed in the Arabic language for a number of important purposes[139] including the ability to shift gracefully between the written word and the experienced word in time and space. God says: "Truly in the creation of the skies and the earth and the alternation of the night and the day are proofs for those with deep understanding" (*Āl ᶜImrān*: 190). Understanding the meanings of the Qur'an, in part or entirety, necessitates some level of proficiency in classical Arabic, though faith is the element that makes the Qur'an comprehensible without which even an Arabic speaker cannot appreciate its meanings. While some differences in dialect are natural and expected given geography, history and culture, the recent emphasis on colloquial Arabic, i.e., the different dialects spoken in different countries, in addition to the proliferation of common expressions not rooted in classical Arabic, especially among youth as expressions of national identity, has challenged common understanding of the message of the Qur'an and has lost sight of the unifying strength of Islam's mother tongue. So significant is the potential role of strengthening the Arabic language in the re-emergence of the Muslim civilization that it warrants a well-researched, resourced and protected policy that must necessarily extend beyond education. Without this priority we can continue to expect the manipulation of people who profess Islam but have a limited capacity to understand it on their own. Arabic language acquisition is arguably an essential objective in its own right.

The mind is not only stimulated by educational and scientific activities. The Shariʿah points to other important areas like the arts, recreation and entertainment. These are seriously understudied areas as jurists have traditionally taken a negative view of anything they deem distracts people from their religious duties. In contrast, the Shariʿah presents these fields as natural human aspirations that actually characterize and ease earthly existence contributing to happiness and wellbeing. Prophet Muhammad was known for his understanding and tolerance in this regard.[140] Warnings against excess are certainly not intended to prohibit the development and enjoyment of the arts, recreation and entertainment.

Preservation of Progeny

The *maqṣad* of the preservation of progeny (*nasl*) originated from what the early scholars considered to be the underlying intent for the punishment of adultery (*zinā*). This is a particularly patriarchal and culturally specific understanding for a punishment that clearly has more to do with preserving public morality than it has to do with knowing a child's lineage. This much is clear from the very strict injunctions associated with accusations of adultery, including the presence of four witnesses who can attest to actually having seen intercourse take place. In other words, a clear violation of public morality must have occurred. Otherwise bringing forth an accusation with compromised evidence constitutes a breach of privacy and warrants punishment of the accuser. If the basis of punishments as the source of the *maqāṣid* is accepted, then the more apt *maqṣad* for this particular punishment should have been the preservation of public morality – an area of universal concern. This is not to say that knowing and protecting biological lineage is unimportant in Islam, which can be dealt with by referring to injunctions related to safeguarding a child's family name in cases of adoption, but it is to draw attention to the importance that the Shariʿah places on people's privacy. The stringent rules related to accusations ensure wide latitude for human behavior and prescribe limits on communal and state intervention in the personal lives of citizens.

Without critiquing its basis, scholars have evolved the preservation of progeny to encompass a broader conception of the family unit. Ibn

Ashur (d. 1973) observed that "… it has been one of the objectives of all laws in the world to take special care of the family by laying down specific rules for its formation and proper functioning."[141] Although Auda observes that it is not clear whether Ibn Ashur was building on the preservation of progeny or replacing it with a new conception, he opened the way for contemporary scholars to rethink this *maqṣid*.[142] The SIP scholars focused their concerns "around the promotion of the well-being of the family unit, including a focus on a healthy marriage and children."[143]

There is no doubt that the family unit is one of the most important social units in any society. The proper functioning of families has serious implications for the well-being of a nation. Family structures, composition and behavior have changed dramatically over the past several decades and this is as true in Muslim communities as it is elsewhere. Better understanding the implications of these changes can help local authorities (both from government and civil society) deal more effectively with a whole host of social challenges that are emerging as a result. The focus on marriage and divorce and the rights of women and children are important aspects of policy, however, policy makers must be willing and courageous enough to address modern anomalies that have become pervasive within family units, i.e., issues resulting from more complex political, social, economic and cultural transformations. Single-motherhood and the intensifying pressures on women to shoulder the burden of child rearing while earning a living needs greater policy attention almost everywhere in the world and particularly in Muslim communities. So too does the unprecedented spike in violence against women worldwide due to wars but also a general attitude of male chauvinism that pervades many Muslim societies and institutions. Much of the violence that Muslim women suffer occurs within the family unit. This is an unacceptable phenomenon from a religious perspective and a serious oversight by the SIP scholars. Indeed, the absence of a single female scholarly voice in the Shariah Index Project is a disconcerting but telling sign.

Preservation of Wealth

The preservation of wealth (*māl*) finds its origins in the punishment for theft. Auda traces the evolution of this objective "into familiar socio-economic terminology, such as 'social assistance,' 'economic development,' 'flow of money,' 'wellbeing of society,' and 'diminishing the difference between economic levels.'"[144] The SIP scholars also observed that this objective was expanded to include "not only the protection of public and private property, but also the integrity of trade and prohibition of all types of unlawful gain."[145] Their discussion focused on the definition of usury and its relationship to modern concepts of interest. Usury is prohibited in Islam and its equation with interest has caused many Islamic thinkers consternation given the dependence of the global capitalist system on usurious transactions. As a way around this prohibition, one SIP participant observed that the definition of usury is "any amount of interest charged which is two percent above the rate of inflation."[146] The idea suggested here is that usury is "lending money at an exorbitant rate of interest."[147] In the final analysis the SIP scholars chose to avoid a definitive pronouncement on the prohibition of all interest. This is an interesting dilemma given the clarity of the Qur'anic prohibition.

The challenge with interest is the complexity and strength of the global financial system versus the dearth of Islamic alternatives. The margin of laxity noted above is not intended to apply to the debt of nations but rather lending policies to individuals and, at most, small businesses. The SIP scholars are, however, talking about governance and policy. This kind of postulating does not acknowledge, reference, or admit the nature of national borrowing and the challenge of debt servicing. When governments borrow money to finance their operations, they repay that money by taking it from taxpayers. Government debt can either be owed to internal or foreign creditors. In both cases those borrowing the money are not the same actors repaying the money – a quandary that is somewhat mitigated in advanced democratic systems where citizens largely benefit from the resulting allocation of resources. Corruption often means that while citizens bear the burden of interest and principal repayments, the benefits largely do not accrue to them. This is not the same relationship alluded to by the SIP scholars where he who takes the debt is responsible for the consequences of repayment. We cannot only consider percentages at the state and interstate levels; we must also consider the magnitude of the principal and how it is employed because that is what will determine the possibility and severity of repayment. It is best to admit that we have failed thus far to offer a viable alternative to the existing financial system than to find ways of easing our conscience and inadvertently encouraging complacency in seeking a more equitable world order.

Of all the conventional *maqāṣid*, the preservation of wealth as an objective of the Shariʿah is perhaps the least defensible. The positive corollary for the punishment for theft is not the preservation of wealth but rather the guarantee and sanctity of human security in all of its dimensions. The severity of the punishment for theft (sadly whose true spirit in terms of strict requirement of social context is often betrayed because it cannot be applied at times of poverty, injustice, inequality etc.) reflects Islam's emphasis on freedom from transgression and violence including that of the state and other actors in positions of power. In stark contrast to the suggestion that wealth is an objective of the Shariʿah, the Qur'an exhorts to the most generous forms of giving and sharing. Much of the concern of the Shariʿah is based on controlling human greed and want for more and how this distracts believers from their ultimate objective. Wealth is and can only ever be a means, not an objective. Wealth in the Qur'an is referred to as both adornment or *zīnah* (*al-Kahf*: 46) and trial or *fitnah* (*al-Anfāl*: 28). Neither can credibly be described as a higher objective of the Shariʿah. Wealth is a means to demonstrate piety and morality. It is a tool for bettering and advancing life; otherwise it is a distraction and test. When ʿUmar ibn al-Khaṭṭāb, the second caliph, refused to divide whole cities and provinces over the Companions as spoils of war, he referred to more general verses of the Qur'an, arguing that God did not will the rich to dominate wealth.[148] If the preservation of wealth and private property were objectives, this decision would not have made sense then or now.

Moreover, the SIP's confident inclusion of intellectual property as part of this understanding is contestable. When Prophet Muhammad decreed: "Three things cannot be denied to anyone: water, pasture and fire,"[149] he was referring to what we call public goods in today's terminology. Knowledge, the subject of intellectual property, is a public good. In other words, our collective use of it will never diminish our individual utilities. In fact, there are arguments to be made that we might all be better off if knowledge was freely available as the SIP scholars argued in their presentation of the preservation of the mind. This does not mean that we are not to reward innovation; it just opines that as Muslim thinkers we must try to find instruments that better reflect the teachings of the Shariʿah and fulfill human welfare. Patents that prevent the poor from access to affordable medicines are not Shariʿah compliant, nor are copyrights that slow the progress or increase the costs of innovation or prevent the publication and affordable dissemination of critical ideas. This discussion draws our attention to the necessity of researching, critiquing and strategizing about global development, trade and financial institutions that may not advance the principles of economic justice noted by the SIP scholars. It also draws our attention to gaps in the classical *maqāṣid* approach.

Preservation of Honour

The preservation of honour is traced back to the punishment for slander (*qadhf*) or breaching honour. In contemporary Islamic Law the concept is being expanded to include 'preservation of human dignity' as well as human rights.[150] The SIP scholars focus on classic notions of human rights within Islamic jurisprudence noting that fundamental rights and liberties are based on humanity rather than national or religious affiliation.[151] According to the scholars, rights that protect honour include: "the right to due process; protection from torture, arbitrary arrest, and detention; protection of privacy (including privacy of home and personal correspondence); protection from discrimination based on race, religion, and gender; and protection against public slander or libel."[152]

The Qur'anic incident that resulted in the application of strict punishment for slander, interestingly reveals other very important objectives of the Shariʿah. Islam's intolerance for slander is more suitably associated with the protection of liberties. In particular, to allow unrelated men and women the liberty of carrying out their affairs within shared communal and social spaces without fear of harm or reproach. On a general level God cautions people about believing what they hear without evidence and then spreading damaging rumors and mischief (*al-Nūr*: 11). In particular, He emphasizes: "Those who accuse honourable but unwary believing women are cursed by God, in this life and the next. A painful punishment awaits them" (*al-Nūr*: 23). The severity of the punishment for slander and the strict evidential requirements serve to affirm and protect a social order that permits women to move about freely without fear of reproach and defamation. In other words, it affirms the agency of women including their freedom of secure movement as well as the necessity of cooperation between the sexes. These allowances have yet to be fully recognized in many Muslim communities and especially among their traditional religious authorities. There is no doubt that women's security is generally compromised worldwide though to varying degrees.

Although women's rights may certainly be subsumed under all the *maqāṣid*, I believe that special mention is mandated in this discussion. No group has been more seriously harmed than women on account of cultural practices that view the preservation of honour as the complete opposite of the explanation presented above. "Honor" killings continue to take place in some Arab Bedouin and Southeast Asian societies unjustly violating the lives and rights of innocent girls and women. The SIP scholars were "emphatic that the cultural practice of 'honor killing' is a false and wrongful application of this *maqṣad* and is a flagrant violation of the sanctity of human life and its clear *maqṣad*."[153] In light of this strong condemnation we need to take an unambiguous stand on the protection of girls and women, something that traditional religious authorities have been unacceptably reluctant to unanimously and unequivocally endorse. We also need to be more assertive in arguing, demanding and enforcing women's rights in the Shariʿah – rights that one may argue is an objective in itself. Organizations that refuse to unconditionally eschew all forms of violence against women must be reprimanded and eventually barred for non-compliance.

Conclusion

The *maqāṣid* approach originated from an understanding of the values that jurists believed to be at the heart of the Shariʿah's strictest penalties. The six objectives outlined above form the most enduring contribution of the approach. The classification of the preservation of religion, life, mind, progeny, wealth and dignity has enjoyed a parsimonious existence that no other *maqāṣid* exposition has surpassed. Evolving the terminology and substance of each *maqṣad* has been an easier feat than presenting new typologies all together. Given this intellectual inertia, contemporary scholarship has attempted to honor a broader and deeper meaning of the Sharīʿah while respecting the approach's well-established roots. The Shariah Index Project is one such attempt. In addition to evolving the substance of each *maqṣad*, the Project has explicitly and completely shifted *maqāṣid* from the realm of law to that of governance. This is a courageous first step despite its shortcomings and challenges.

That said, the *maqāṣid* approach continues to exhibit a solitary life playing out on the margins of Islamic academe and struggling to attract deserved attention. Elevating the *maqāṣid* from its subordinate position within the traditional religious establishment continues to be a daunting task. According to contemporary *maqāṣid* scholars the approach remains on the margins of mainstream scholarship and has yet to contribute to other disciplines. Kamali observes "even to this day, many reputable text books on the science of the sources of law (*uṣūl al-fiqh*) do not mention the *maqāṣid* in their list of usual topics. Similarly, although they are embedded within discussions of ijtihad [juridical reasoning], the *Maqāṣid* have often not been treated as such in conventional descriptions of the theory of *ijtihad*."[154] According to Attia, "legal studies have exhibited only limited interest in *maqāṣid* and goals."[155]

Undoubtedly, part of the reluctance to fully embrace *maqāṣid* by traditional scholars is due to its perceived discretionary nature. Thus, while some acknowledge the *maqāṣid* as a critical approach and tool for Islamic reform, others view it as abstract, subjective and non-verifiable rhetoric. Irrespective, even in its traditional form, the *maqāṣid* approach helps to stimulate discussion as well as to bridge the gap between Islamic law and governance, and for that we owe it greater attention.

4

The Challenges of Founding a New Discipline

Truly, God loves that if any of you performs a task that you should master it.

PROPHET MUHAMMAD[156]

The parsimonious nature of the traditional *maqāṣid* approach as embodied in the preservation of the six objectives – religion, life, mind, progeny, wealth and dignity – appears to resonate widely with students of public policy and governance. It is not difficult to see this inherently legal theory as one that is readily applicable to policy, governance and potentially other social sciences. The shift from law to governance including but not limited to the integration of Islamic economics, however, must be scrutinized with the aspiration of achieving greater academic as well as practical rigour. Undoubtedly, this is the key to building a new and relevant discipline that could contribute to policy studies while integrating and benefiting from the religious insights that have been elaborated over centuries in the *maqāṣid* literature. This chapter focuses the spotlight on some of the more salient challenges of advancing a genuine project in public policy and governance in Islam.

To this end, it is divided into four major parts. The first examines how Shariᶜah and fiqh are customarily understood versus their actual meanings. The second part discusses methodological concepts that can be adapted from the fundamentals of fiqh or *uṣūl al-fiqh* and others that must be rejected for the construction of a robust intellectual foundation relevant to public policy in Islam. This leads to a discussion in the third part of the contemporary contributions of two renowned scholars whose contributions to *maqāṣid*, ethics, fiqh and *uṣūl al-fiqh* are relevant for this project. Finally, the fourth part of this chapter highlights the requirements of governance and policy studies.

The Shariʿah of God and the Fiqh of Man

The robustness of any discipline is based on the strength and credibility of its source materials and evidence. In Islamic studies the most important source by far is the Qur'an and Sunnah as the former's preeminent illustration. Together these provide the foundations for our knowledge of the Shariʿah. The Shariʿah is commonly understood to mean law, way, or a way of life. As the ordinance or higher law established by God, the Shariʿah represents the righteous path given the incalculable parameters of life at any given moment. This path is not delimited to individuals but equally applies to larger social units including governing authorities. The Shariʿah proper can only be understood through a thorough investigation of Revealed and unrevealed knowledge or the written and unwritten word. The result of this process nevertheless can only ever constitute fiqh, not the Shariʿah itself whose laws are unchanging and to which the potential application of intellectual effort is infinite. Generally, fiqh is an understanding of the Shariʿah that usually, but not necessarily, is based on an established methodology.

The word Shariʿah only occurs once in the Qur'an though there are words with the same root, *sha-ra-ʿa,* with similar import, none of which refer to the legal system that developed much later. In its first mention, *shirʿah*, the term is used to describe the *direction* that God created for each community of believers and its attendant means or *minhāj* for each to reach their respective goal (5:48). We are told that if God had willed, He would have made us one community but instead He wished to test each with what it has received. The primary idea is that every community excels beyond the other in doing good from their vantage given their divinely ordained way. According to Ibn Ashur, "... humankind has never lacked good practices that are the result of Divine laws or good advice or sound minds. Thus, the Arabs were inheritors of the *ḥanīfiyyah*, the Jews were heirs of the Great Laws of Moses, and the Christians were inheritors of both Mosaic Law and the teachings of Jesus."[157]

This is very important for governance as it establishes the understanding that each community is entitled to struggle in its unique way using the means that God has furnished for it based on its intrinsic characteristics. This does not preclude one religion or *Dīn* but provides for different paths depending on a people's *shirᶜah* and *minhāj* by which they are expected to advance all that is good.

The second form of the root *sha-ra-ᶜa* in the Qur'an is *sharaᶜa* which means ordained. God has *ordained* for us from the Religion that which He advised Noah, Abraham, Moses and Jesus and that which He inspired to Muhammad so that they may together establish the Religion and not become divided therein (*al-Shūrā*: 13). Thus, it is a common Religion with multiple paths and means. Another form of *sha-ra-ᶜa* follows closely in reference to those who deny the Hereafter and wish only for the gains of this world. In this instance the Qur'an asks "Do they have partners who have ordained (*sharaᶜū*) for them from the Religion what was not permitted by God?" (*al-Shūrā*: 21). Thus, it is only God who has the power to ordain the higher law that believers ought to follow and it is each individual's role to internalize, contextualize, and express this law for the advancement of life.

The only reference to the Shariᶜah proper in the Qur'an is associated with Prophet Muhammad. "Then We put you upon an exemplary or higher law or ordinance (*sharīᶜah*) from the Command, so follow it and do not follow the whims of those who do not know" (*al-Jāthiyah*: 18). Auda thus asserts that the Shariᶜah is "the revelation that Muhammad had received and made practicing it the message and mission of his life, i.e., the Qur'an and Prophetic tradition."[158] Abdul Rauf confers with this explanation noting: "In its widest and most inclusive sense, the term shari'ah refers to the Divine Ordinances, the set of laws ordained by God the Lawgiver (Shaari') for all humankind ..."[159]

The methodological consequences for policy and governance of an explicit expansion of our understanding of the Shariᶜah to include all Revealed and unrevealed knowledge have yet to be expounded. The possibilities for new understandings of the Shariᶜah that are purposeful, unifying, and holistic while encompassing dynamism are infinite. For instance, the approach to Qur'anic exegesis would most closely conform to Hasan al-Turabi's conceptualization in *al-Tafsīr al-Tawḥīdī* (The Unifying Exegesis) where he states:

> On the level of language, it entails 'dealing with the Qur'anic language as an integral whole' and 'unifying the language of the Qur'an with the language of the receivers of the message at the time of the revelation.' On the level of human knowledge, it entails a holistic approach to both the unseen and seen worlds with all their multitude of components and rules that govern them. On the level of topics, it entails dealing with themes regardless of the order of verses, in addition to applying them to everyday life. In terms of scope, it has to include people regardless of their space and time. It also entails unifying law with morality and spirituality in one holistic approach.[160]

These insights demand the birth of a new fiqh that takes governance and policy as well as the challenges of our times as its explicit focus.

As a Qur'anic concept, fiqh generally means understanding or comprehension. In almost every mention in the Qur'an this is the primary meaning of the word. There is only one instance where fiqh is intended to convey the more specific meaning of a deep understanding of religion for the purpose of conveying it to others (*al-Tawbah*: 122). Within religious circles, fiqh has taken on a more exclusive meaning of "knowledge of practical revealed rulings extracted from detailed evidences."[161] Fiqh has thus been mistakably limited to "the huge collection of juridical opinions that were given by various jurists from various schools of thought, in regards to the application of Shariʿah to their various real life situations throughout the past fourteen centuries."[162]

The *maqāṣid* approach for governance and policy makes very significant contributions to fiqh in this regard. Because the approach distinguishes between means that can 'expire' over time or with a change in context and the ends that remain timeless,[163] radical re-interpretations and the historicizing of fiqh as it concerns human dealings while maintaining the integrity of the Shariʿah becomes possible and necessary. In this way, researchers are required to "attend to the changing circumstances in which such declarations [establishing the bases of essential interests] are made."[164] Any path which achieves the objectives of the Shariʿah in substance and process is worthy of consideration.[165] In essence, while the Shariʿah is unchanging, its understanding is dynamic.

We cannot proceed to examine modern issues of governance and policy without this affirmation. Our knowledge of today's realities must augment, enhance and correct understandings of the past. Whether we accept the traditional *maqāṣid* classification of the preservation of religion, life, mind, progeny, wealth and dignity or we include contemporary contributions that emphasize the preservation of the earth, peaceful co-existence, advancement of human well-being and the elimination of corruption, as well as the incorporation of justice, equality, freedom and social, economic and political rights, the *maqāṣid* present an invaluable approach to improving our current state of human affairs.

Reconsidering Certain Methodological Concepts

A *maqāṣid* approach to policy and governance will by necessity reconsider four critical concepts commonly accepted in traditional fiqh. Fiqh is predominantly based on *āyāt al-aḥkām* or the legislative verses of the Qur'an as well as Prophetic narrations with legislative content. This naturally limits the evidences from which the traditional *maqāṣid* were derived. Because of this, the Qur'an is greatly underutilized, analyzed and understood. Yet properly understanding the Qur'an is perhaps the single most important contributor to building a robust edifice for studies in policy and governance. A holistic approach to the Shariʿah is simply not possible in the absence of a comprehensive incorporation of Qur'anic content as well as the Sunnah that directly pertains to an elaboration of its meanings.

Policy and governance studies also demand a reconsideration of popular juridical theories of Islamic law. While a number of the approaches used by the various schools can be of relevance to governance and policy, scholars still have the task of defining these techniques in ways that reflect the needs of the discipline. Content and processes related to consensus, the determination of benefits, blocking the means, preference and analogy will have to find their roots in the needs of governance, which has different concerns and constraints. Moreover, normative judgments related to customs, continuity and the Companions' opinions also have to be mitigated by knowledge of the policy sciences. In other words, these methods will necessarily have to be defined and applied in ways that contribute to policy and governance.

In light of this, evidences and their outcomes must be articulated and demonstrated within cultural, social and political contexts. Marshalling support from fragmented and isolated evidences no matter how numerous and whether originating in the primary sources or from the body of fiqh already in existence will not lead to the outcomes suggested by the *maqāṣid*. Al-Shāṭibī's insistence that the process of induction infuses the *maqāṣid* with complete certitude is simply not verifiable without an understanding of context and environmental interdependencies. No ruling can hope to achieve desired outcomes without alignment or compatibility with other elements in the system. The importance of support factors that must be in place to ensure that a ruling, decision or policy is beneficial cannot be underestimated. In essence the success of every rule is associated with a causal principle that cannot possibly be isolated from the broader context within which it is embedded.

Consequently, the *maqāṣid* approach cannot admit the *fiqhī* concept of abrogation. To abrogate a verse or several means to cancel them out with the justification that their literal meaning contradicts with that of a later verse. However, disagreements over interpretation may be due to "surrounding circumstances, such as war and peace, poverty and wealth, urban and rural life, summer and winter, sickness and health, or young and old."[166] Auda explains that "... a large number of evidences are cancelled, one way or another, for no good reason other than that the jurists' failing to understand how they could fit them in a unified perceptual framework."[167] Abrogating verses due to a lack of contextual understanding is unacceptable and highly subjective. In addition to an already narrow approach to the Shariʿah, traditional jurisprudents lose even more of the source material through this arbitrary device. In the final analysis, there is no support for this concept in the Qur'an or Sunnah[168] and scholars are exhorted to respect the comprehensive and holistic integrity of both.

Similarly, a *maqāṣid* approach to governance cannot unequivocally support the notion of the *silence* of the Lawgiver. According to al-Raysuni, "it is a recognized fact that the Lawgiver may remain silent on certain matters or rulings due to the absence of an occasion or cause for further declarations. As a result the door is open to independent reasoning and interpretations and analogical deduction."[169] Many draw on the Prophet's saying: "God has set up boundaries, so do not transgress them; He kept silent on certain things out of mercy to you rather than forgetfulness so do not ask about them."[170] While this is intended, as al-Hibri correctly asserts, "not to regulate every part of Muslims' lives,"[171] there are two important concerns. The first is the determination of silence when so much of the Shariʿah is not part of the body of *āyāt al-aḥkām* referenced by the scholars not to mention the complete neglect of unrevealed knowledge in the natural and social sciences. While this has given rise to the concept of unrestricted interests or *al-maṣāliḥ al-mursalah* "which are recognized by Islamic Law but which are not mentioned by name in any of the particular legal texts"[172] and therefore include the *maqāṣid* and spinoff disciplines like *siyāsah sharʿiyyah* or Shariʿah-oriented policy, it has also facilitated an unjustified neglect within these approaches of studying the entirety of the Shariʿah. As we expand the source material to include all of the Qur'anic text and authentic hadith with verified content, while applying more complex methodologies, perceptions of the silence of the Law Giver necessarily change. Indeed, the Qur'an states: "... We have not neglected anything in the Book..." (*al-Anʿām*: 38). A *maqāṣid* approach to policy and governance studies cannot be limited to *āyāt al-aḥkām* or the epistemological restrictions of the fundamentals of jurisprudence (*uṣūl al-fiqh*). The Shariʿah is much more encompassing and accommodating than either concedes.

The second concern with the assertion of silence is related to time and place as well as the expertise of the scholar. The Qur'an is a dynamic text and the fluidity of the Revealed and unrevealed word cannot be overlooked. As the Qur'an is approached in different times and places by different individuals and groups, considerations of silence are likely to change. In other words, silence that is alleged by one generation based on interpretative and integrative capacities may be contested by the next as the state of knowledge inevitably changes.

The growing complexity of the state of knowledge draws attention to another characteristic of traditional fiqh that the *maqāṣid* approach for governance and policy will have to reconsider, namely reliance on individual jurists as opposed to collective and transdisciplinary expertise. Through an exploration of the Revealed and unrevealed significance of the Qur'anic injunction of *shūrā* or collective decision-making it is clear that public affairs must be deliberated and decided collectively in accordance with the public interest and the most advanced state of human knowledge concerning any specific issue. By alluding to the criticality of engaging epistemic communities, as well as knowledgeable and interested stakeholders, *shūrā* is intended to greatly diminish uncertainty. Greater certitude becomes possible only when we share our understandings of how the Revealed and unrevealed word combine to produce new and useful knowledge that can be brought to bear on the challenges of the moment.

Contemporary Reform Efforts

I have chosen to highlight two contemporary approaches to Islamic intellectual reform in this chapter on account of their useful insights for policy and governance. Although they are not in opposition of each other, the approaches of Tariq Ramadan and Jasser Auda present different emphases. Ramadan argues that "the concepts and geography of the sources of *uṣūl al-fiqh* must certainly be reconsidered. It cannot be enough to rely on scriptural sources to examine the relationship between human knowledge (religion, philosophy, the experimental and human sciences, etc.) and applied ethics: the Universe, Nature, and the knowledge related to them must assuredly be integrated into the process through which the higher objectives and ethical goals (*al-maqāṣid*) of Islam's general message can be established."[173] The sources of *uṣūl al-fiqh* must integrate all human knowledge, of the natural and social sciences, "into the ethical finalities of Islam's message."[174]

Ramadan relies on three basic distinctions that he argues have been obscured in Islamic thought to support his propositions: the immutable versus the changing; principles versus models; and worship versus human dealings. "So long as they [rationality, creativity and research] remain faithful to the principles and respect prohibitions, their intellectual, scientific, artistic, and more generally, social, economic, and political productions are not innovations, but instead welcome achievements for welfare of humankind."[175] Both the Revealed text, which "opens manifold, diverse horizons for the exercise of an autonomous active rationality"[176] as well as the practice of the early Companions and community of believers who exhibited a "constant to-and-fro movement between the texts and the intentions and habits" of their immediate environment attest to the credibility of this assertion.[177] As with the text, the universe reveals immutable laws while others are "contextual, changing and immersed in history..."[178] In this way, Ramadan's work is reminiscent of the late renowned scholar Taha Jabir Alalwani who in his proposal for the foundations of a contemporary ijtihad suggested that "our understanding of religion and religious practice should, in the first instance, be based on the study of Divine Revelation on the one hand, and the real dynamic world on the other. The Qur'an guides us to the marvels and secrets of the physical world while reflection on the real world leads us back to understanding the Qur'an."[179]

Today the growing complexity of the natural and human sciences has made the task of jurists particularly challenging. The knowledge gap between the texts and contexts is widening exponentially and the outcomes are evident in the growing irrelevance of Islamic participation in fora beyond the strict confines of traditional fiqh and *uṣūl al-fiqh*. Increasingly, jurists are expected to give opinions or pass judgments on issues of which they have little knowledge where they are forced to rely on outside expertise (if indeed they perceive a need to consult at all). Most *fuqahā'* councils solicit the views of scientists or specialists in specific fields requiring technical expertise. This reliance has not been reflected in the social sciences where "consultations remain marginal and superficial."[180] The *fuqahā'*, according to Ramadan, consider these disciplines "too approximate."[181] For Ramadan, as for many other scholars, this is not acceptable. He argues that "those different fields do provide perspectives that are important to know and that seem necessary to integrate into the elaboration of ethical norms orienting individual and collective human behavior" and that "each field of knowledge necessarily lays out its own methods, rules, and analysis and experimentation norms autonomously according to its area of study."[182]

While commendable, this position does not recognize the epistemic challenges and contestable authorities within these fields and the likelihood that they are not developed with a unification or *tawḥīdī* philosophy. In its essence *tawḥīd* encompasses the oneness of God. On a more sophisticated level it expresses the covenant between human beings and God not to sever what He commanded to be joined (*al-Baqarah*: 27). The implications of this demand are not limited to the social sciences. The development of the natural sciences in ways that have denied the existence of God, the interconnectedness of all creation and the role of spirituality necessitate critique and caution on the part of anyone working from within an Islamic framework. Just as the *fuqahā'* are being criticized for their limited expertise in *worldly* affairs, so too is criticism warranted of those who have stripped the social and natural sciences of their fundamental essence and relation to the Shariʿah.

Ramadan's assertion that "the text sciences are not more 'Islamic' than the sciences of the Universe" is an unacceptable stretch if what he means by the sciences of the universe is the way scholars have understood them as opposed to how God has created them.[183] The texts have a clear unquestionable direction – we cannot reach a conclusion of disbelief from the texts (unless we deny what is written) whereas those who study science void of God often do reach conclusions of disbelief especially in our modern age of hyper-rationality. A *maqāṣid* approach to governance and policy insists that text and context cannot be fully understood in isolation of one another. The *combined reading* articulated by Alalwani in which "a reading of Revelation for an understanding of the physical world and its laws and principles, and a reading of the physical world to appreciate and recognize the value of Revelation" addresses this concern.[184]

With this oversight, Ramadan proposes that authority in the Islamic universe must shift to reflect the expertise and competence of the scholars of context (*ʿulamāʾ al-wāqiʿ*). In other words, the scholars of the text and the scholars of the context must work on an "equal footing."[185] This can be accomplished by integrating "those specialists (scientists or experts) with the best mastery of contemporary scientific knowledge within their specialties and the research techniques related to them" into the "circles of text scholars during their debates and deliberations to formulate legal rulings, the *fatāwā* about specific issues."[186] The former must therefore be acknowledged as *ʿulamāʾ al-wāqiʿ* specializing in the context, on equal par with *ʿulamāʾ al-nuṣūṣ* specializing in the text. Ramadan concludes that in order to effect *radical reform* in the Islamic sciences:

> It is urgent to devise *equal-representation*, *egalitarian*, and *specialized research* and *fatwa* committees that are able to ally three essential requirements: global understanding of the two Books' higher goals, awareness of the higher objectives and goal in their field of study (the texts or writings in a particular scientific field), and first hand specialized knowledge in the said subject (*fuqahāʾ* specializing in texts related to medicine, economics, and other fields – according to the committee in question – being naturally associated with scientists dealing with the same field).[187]

This appears to equate two unqualified endeavors and it is not obvious how either side can benefit from the other or produce a truly radical outcome while each side has approached its field of expertise with little if anything of what the other side has internalized as truth. In other words, without studying the texts with governance and policy lenses the jurist will not perceive in the texts what is relevant to that field and thus can only bring to the table what he or she is capable of seeing in the first place. Similarly, the scientist's lack of experience with the texts not only disables him or her from correcting or enhancing the text scholars understanding, but also impacts the ultimate truths of his expertise and what he can legitimately contribute to an Islamic perspective. The economic sciences, for instance, that

Ramadan suggests must be studied in order to develop "an applied Islamic ethics in economics" cannot possibly enable us to achieve this goal, which is something that he clearly acknowledges further in his book.[188] The god of conventional economics is an idol, an object of material admiration, capitalism is its religion and profits are its only goal. In contrast, Islamic economics has yet to articulate a viable and unified framework that can provide policy makers with the evidence, tools and strategies necessary for social justice and democratic governance but more significantly that can contend with current capitalist structures. As the hegemonic discipline in the policy sciences today, Islamic economics is very far from providing this alternative for public policy in Islam.

The key then is not to elevate and equate individuals, however their expertise is contestably defined, but to shift the levels of authority associated with ideas and sources of evidence as they express, reinforce and reproduce the objectives of the Shariʿah. It is not to view the Revelation and Universe as "two books" as Ramadan suggests[189] but to view them as one book that demands "two readings" that are underlain with the values of monotheism (*tawḥīd*), purification (*tazkiyah*), and civilization (*ʿumrān*) as Alalwani suggests.[190] Expertise in understanding one form of the Revelation without an understanding of the other is simply not possible.

As part of Auda's proposed classification for theories of Islamic law, he suggests "a shift in the 'levels of authority' from the usual binary categorization of valid/invalid evidences into a multi-level 'spectrum' of validity of evidences and sources."[191] Auda includes in these sources the rich heritage of traditional jurisprudence, interests (*maṣāliḥ)*, rational arguments and modern declarations of rights as well as the outputs of modern tendencies in various contemporary theories of Islamic law. Auda, like Ramadan, insists on the incorporation of the natural and social sciences without which he argues that "research in the fundamental theory of Islamic law will remain within the limits of traditional literature and its manuscripts, and Islamic law will continue to be largely 'outdated' in its theoretical bases and practical outcomes."[192] He encourages the use of science where applicable, e.g., determination of legal capacity and in differentiating between the different stages of life.[193] Also like Ramadan, Auda stops short of conditioning the inclusion of any such knowledge on adherence to the Islamic precept of unification or *tawḥīd*, overlooking the normative character of knowledge. Unlike Ramadan, however, Auda's main concern is not with the incorporation of knowledge of the Universe into the circles of *fuqahā'* but rather to critique and reform the theory of *uṣūl* itself.

Utilizing a systems approach, Auda proposes the *maqāṣid* as a *philosophy of Islamic law*. His aim is to develop a theory that "will build on the analysis of sources, implications, and evidences in classic theories, the literature of the schools of Islamic law endorsed by traditionalists, new modernist re-interpretations, and the criticism presented by the post-modernists."[194] Taking five selective features of systems including cognition, holism, openness, multi-dimensionality and purposefulness, Auda both critiques and offers suggestions for reforming Islamic law. The feature of cognition differentiates between what is Divinely Revealed versus the understanding of the jurist. From this perspective, "rulings are what the jurist judges to be most probably true, and different juridical opinions are all valid expressions of the truth(s) and are all correct."[195] While this may relieve the intensity of violence of disagreement among scholars it is hardly an ethical position. The fact of the matter is, different juridical opinions are not all valid, credible or ethical and we must have the courage to characterize them as such.

Holism contributes to a better understanding of the limits of causation in Islamic law. While traditional jurisprudents had perceived the main issue with single evidences to be certainty versus uncertainty, Auda draws our attention to the "prime problem of single-evidenced approach, which is the partiality and atomism of its 'causation' basis."[196] Auda uses the feature of holism to demonstrate that any phenomenon can potentially be attributable to a number of causes in addition to which we must strive to recognize and emphasize purpose. Indeed, evidence-based policy making considers purposes, causes and a whole host of support factors that ultimately lead to the outcome observed.

As for openness, Auda suggests that Islamic law can benefit from two mechanisms. The first involves changing rulings with changes in the worldview of the jurist. This will decrease literalism and allow for the integration of the natural and social sciences in the system of Islamic law. The second involves "openness to philosophical investigation, which evolves with the evolution of human knowledge, in general."[197] While these are necessary developments for jurists, the exclusive focus on jurists is concerning. There needs to develop an openness within the Islamic sciences to multi-disciplinary experts who combine enough knowledge of the primary sources, their discipline as well as the necessary faith to make valuable contributions to humanity in the name of Islam. The need for greater acceptance of pluralism and collective decision-making in these knowledge production processes cannot be overemphasized.

Multidimensionality addresses the challenges of binary thinking that have characterized the schools of Islamic law. Instead of defining concepts in relation to their binary opposite, multidimensionality suggests a spectrum of probability in between the extremes of certain and uncertain. Auda suggests that the combination of this feature with a *maqāṣidī* approach can resolve the "dilemma of opposing evidences." The initial appearance of the contradiction of evidences is largely resolvable with a consideration of contexts or the multidimensional nature of those evidences. Thus, the different rulings that potentially contradictory evidences give rise to actually confirm a shared and overriding objective.

The most fundamental feature of systems thinking, however, that Auda wishes to impress, is purposefulness. This feature is the common link among all other basic system features.[198] The *maqāṣid* are considered the purposes of Islamic law. As such, they are the common link among the different areas of *uṣūl al-fiqh*. A purposeful interpretation of the primary sources, especially as expressed by the 'thematic exegesis school' addresses the Qur'an as a unified whole. "Based on this holistic approach, the small number of verses related to rulings ... will extend from a few hundred verses to the entire text of the Qur'an. Chapters and verses addressing faith, prophets' stories, the hereafter, and nature, will then all comprise parts of a holistic picture and, thus, play a role in shaping juridical rulings." [199] Purposefulness, in other words, allows us to reclaim the entire Shariʿah as our source of ijtihad.

The systems approach suggested by Auda must be explored further. His use of systems theory to posit *maqāṣid* as a philosophy of Islamic law thereby reconciling a diverse range of perspectives, can be usefully employed to study and interpret the primary sources for governance and policy. Indeed, while a theory of governance is not readily presented in the Qur'an in the form of the unified system, it still presents all the "necessary and sufficient elements to construct one."[200] In other words, systems philosophy can itself be applied to studying the Qur'an and Sunnah, as opposed to merely classifying fiqh. In this case, systems philosophy is not used to demonstrate the *maqāṣid* as a philosophy of law *ex post* but rather becomes the foundation of a new method whereby those *maqāṣid* can be determined through a thorough investigation of system elements in the Revealed and unrevealed word.

Both the works of Ramadan and Auda offer useful insights for the development of a *maqāṣid* approach to policy and governance. Their proposals, however, stop short of offering robust approaches that actually integrate the Revealed and unrevealed word in a credible and consistent manner, something that will be necessary for the advancement of this new field. Neither offers sufficient if any critique of the state and tendencies in the natural and social sciences, which limit the importability of their outcomes into a framework that aims to satisfy the objectives of the Shariʿah. We need, as Ramadan insists, to incorporate a broad range of expertise but knowledge produced with the conscious dismissal of the Revealed word cannot be complete or fully credible from an Islamic perspective. Although this is of greater concern in the social sciences, and especially governance, it is no less important in the natural sciences. Systems thinking offers great potential for policy and governance in Islam, but Auda does not take his work far enough to offer us a viable methodology for approaching the primary texts. Undoubtedly, systems theory can make important contributions in analyzing the texts by revealing new knowledge and answering universal questions that are invariably expressed in a number of disciplines. Such a method might offer us the ability to move seamlessly from the Revealed and unrevealed word given their inextricable nature and the enabling potential of systems thinking.

The Requirements of Governance and Policy Studies

Scholars of governance and policy must seek to go beyond fiqh and *siyāsah sharʿiyyah* as it is traditionally understood to develop and apply a suitable *maqāṣid* approach. Such an approach can potentially draw upon all Revealed and unrevealed knowledge to understand the relevant guidance in any policy area, including both substantive and procedural issues as proposed in the works of Ramadan and Auda. The aim is to develop an objective and purposeful approach that can make reasoned contributions to governance and policy. By expanding fiqh to encompass all Revealed and unrevealed knowledge, a *maqāṣid* approach to policy can augment a decision-makers limits while giving greater assurance that what is derived from the primary sources will actually lead to intended objectives. The multidisciplinary nature of this ambition demands a rejection of the superficial boundaries that have thus far prevented fiqh from incorporating critical, and nonetheless credible, insights from a more holistic definition of the Shariʿah.

Siyāsah sharʿiyyah or Shariʿah-oriented policy would not then, as Kamali suggests, be "guided by the guidelines of the *maqāṣid*" as they are currently elaborated but rather the determination of the *maqāṣid* themselves for policy and governance demands a renewed approach. To utilize the classical *maqāṣid* as guidelines in policy and governance is to perpetually generate undifferentiated studies along the lines of the Shariah Index Project.[201] In that effort the six objectives were presented as a classification and justification tool for already existing policies. The policies themselves, however, were not subject to critical scrutiny, nor were there any proposals for new policies that could better address public problems. This is due to the general acceptance that while the classical *maqāṣid* offer "epistemological guidelines," as Kamali suggests, they do not offer "thematic and substantive details, metrics and yardsticks on particular subjects."[202] This means that the ultimate definition of each *maqṣid* is not clear in the different spheres to which they can potentially be applied. A renewed *maqāṣid* methodology to the primary sources, however, would not leave matters so ambiguous and would position the *maqāṣid* at the forefront of the policy process.

Our task is to develop this renewed methodology to study the primary sources, and in particular the Qur'an, in search for all references that inform us about the objectives, rules, relationships, practices and processes of policy and governance. The key would not be a piecemeal approach that serves to "identify which aspects of siyasah, if any, is wanting of adjustment in light of *maqāṣid*, and finally come up with a different reading of that aspect of siyasah,"[203] as Kamali suggests, but rather to revisit the sources using a more appropriate methodology to holistically, purposefully and dynamically determine what they convey about policy and governance. Relatedly, our immediate task is not to "identify, in *tafsīr* and hadith, for instance, reports and interpretations that may be weak and erroneous, and in regards to ijtihad also the strength and weakness of evidence on which it may be founded – or indeed the need, as the case may be, to depart from that ijtihad due to subsequent change of conditions and developments of knowledge"[204] though that may be a byproduct of our efforts. Our primary concern must be directed at the Qur'an and Sunnah.

Much of the productions of the past as well as more contemporary contributions locked in this traditional intellectual framework cannot possibly address the complexities of modern governance especially as they neglected useful lessons from a broader Qur'anic reading and the early history of Islam. Even an interactive reading of fiqh, *siyāsah* and *maqāṣid* as presented by the world renowned Islamic jurist and scholar Yusuf al-Qardawi is relatively weak in the face of real-world and expert knowledge of the policy sciences.[205] Al-Qaradawi undoubtedly proposes important insights into fiqh that include what he terms the jurisprudence of (1) priorities, (2) balances and trade-offs, and (3) change. The limitations of fiqh, *siyāsah* and *maqāṣid* combined with an inadequate recognition of the complexities of modern policy making and governance, however, lead al-Qaradawi to explain these concepts in simplistic ways. For instance, the suggestion that state officials block the entry and import of luxury items when there is a shortage of basic goods neglects that these are different markets with different producers and consumers, not to mention the constraints of global trade regimes and reciprocity.[206] Aside from the fact that the wealthy will obtain these products overseas and thus deprive the government of tax revenues, trade in these items permits growth in other goods and services upon which the enjoyment of these goods depends. Such growth may support the provision of basic goods and employment. Moreover, ownership of a number of luxury items entails the payment of zakat which also supports those in need. In sum, the decision is not so clear-cut and there are many parameters that have to be considered. Deprivation of one will not necessarily translate into provision of the other and may even compromise efforts.

Looking to *siyāsah* or fiqh for such major policy issues even when guided by *maqāṣid* is unjustifiable given the dearth of modern policy-oriented studies in those fields and the way in which elemental knowledge in those fields has been developed. Successful governance today rarely involves a one-way decision-making process where policies are elaborated hierarchically, from superiors to their subordinates, or from the centre to the peripheries. In other words, the dominant methods and processes of traditional fiqh of independent, partial, isolated, top-down and command style decision-making will not work. Instead, there is a need for deliberative processes especially if we respect relevant Islamic injunctions.

The almost complete absence of a major, coherent and modern work on the exploration of governance and public policy from scriptural sources has opened a governance vacuum in Islamic scholarship. In the absence of a well-developed alternative, *maqāṣid* scholars presenting traditional views will increasingly be called upon to fit the approach to a whole host of public concerns without the necessary level of introspection or knowledge required. Although this is eminently preferable to the uncritical importation of archaic legal rulings, the approach (as it currently stands) is far from robust as a theory of governance and indeed does not fully capture the essence of Islam. A renewed exploration of the Shariʿah is required: one that will seek a better understanding of power relations and other human tendencies, decision-making structures, the role of the state and values including accountability, integrity and transparency, in addition to the nature of rights and freedoms. This will necessarily build on what so many eminent scholars, from the past and present, have already achieved but more importantly will draw upon the wealth of knowledge in the primary sources.

Conclusion

The advancement of public policy and governance in Islam will undoubtedly demand the creation of a robust intellectual foundation. Reconceptualizing the Shariʿah, expanding fiqh, incorporating multi-disciplinary expertise, critically approaching the classic *maqāṣid* and developing a new methodology that incorporates all of these necessities are some of the more salient challenges. This chapter argued that certain methodological concepts can be useful for this project while others must be reconsidered or rejected. It also considered the potential contribution of two contemporary scholars, Ramadan and Auda, whose insights, along with other illustrious scholars mentioned throughout this book, can form a starting point for the development of an interesting, lively and highly relevant field of study. With these pioneers as our guides, we must nevertheless have the courage and capacity to critique based on new approaches to the primary sources of the Qur'an and Sunnah, which persistently present true seekers of knowledge with renewed and potentially new objectives, rules, relationships, practices and processes that are relevant to policy and governance for our times.

III
Rights and Ethics

5

Human Rights as the Binding Fabric of the *Maqāṣid* for Governance

> We dignified the children of Adam and carried them in the land and the sea; and granted them from all that is good and fair; and preferred them over much of what We created with notable preference.
>
> *AL-ISRĀ'*: 70

Human rights and traditional Islamic scholarship have always been uncomfortable bedmates. Much of what has been written and consequently taught about the Shariʿah does not deal adequately with the issue of human rights. According to Auda "the compatibility of human rights and Islam is a topic of heated debate, both in Islamic and international circles."[207] Implementation of the rulings or *aḥkām* of the Shariʿah are uncritically assumed to provide human rights without the need to elaborate a separate and comprehensive theory or even to test this hypothesis. Many scholars prefer to evade direct confrontation with the issue by couching it in terms of human development,[208] while those who have tackled the issue head-on have yet to articulate an indigenous theory.[209]

This chapter argues that the *maqāṣid* approach to policy and governance centralizes human rights. The rule of the early caliphs is indisputably permeated by safeguarding the rights of their subjects. In fact, governance was largely perceived as an enterprise in custodianship which entailed deep responsibility for all living creatures within the geographic boundaries under the ruler's authority. In the expression of Abū Bakr, first caliph, "The weak amongst you shall be strong with me until I have secured his rights, if God wills; and the strong amongst you shall be weak with me until I have wrested from him the rights of others, if God wills."[210] The gradual abandonment of this priority by Muslim rulers has not only perverted justice but the very essence of Islamic governance. The hesitance of many traditional Islamic scholars to make unequivocal statements regarding human rights has only exacerbated the ensuing crisis.

Our first task is therefore to examine the previous state of the affair. In part one, I present four major reasons for the traditional establishment's reluctance to make clear pronouncements on human rights. The lack of an indigenous approach inevitably contributed to a superficial imitation of global human rights instruments, albeit in *Islamic* guise, which is the focus of part two. Part three examines how the *maqāṣid* literature has attempted to address this shortcoming. The work of *maqāṣid* scholars can be classified in four ways including (1) evolutionary; (2) foundational; (3) interest-based; and (4) complementary. The chapter's main contribution, however, lies in its reconsideration of human rights in Islam. Based on a comprehensive reading of the Qur'an, I argue that the development of an indigenous theory must recognize the categorization of human rights as a fundamental and separate element in the Shariʿah, that such rights are necessarily supply oriented promoting maximal provision, guided by the concept of human dignity, guaranteed through obligations and duties, and rewarded both in this life and the next, i.e., subject to sanction. The universality of this system is found in its non-discriminatory nature of provision. Acceptance of the approach's specificities, however, are necessarily based on accepting Islam as a religion.

A Distressingly Timid Discourse

Muslim scholars have largely been sidetracked from a genuinely original intellectual project related to human rights on account of their preoccupation with the western secular system and what they perceive to be its outcomes. Their concerns can be classified into four major categories. The first concerns the juxtaposition of the Divine versus the secular approach to human rights and who is legitimately subject to either. "The principal difference," argues Kamali "which distinguishes the Shari'ah from secular jurisprudence is that the former subscribes to the overriding authority of Divine Revelation as the determinant of basic moral and legal values."[211] In light of this perception, scholars have expended considerable effort articulating the limits and constraints that they perceive such values place on the rights and associated freedoms articulated in secular systems. In Kamali's exploration of freedom of expression, for instance, he states that legal and moral restraints "occupy a much larger portion of this volume."[212] Given its Divine source and the restrictions that it places on people, a related dilemma with human rights in Islam stems from the determination of the status of disbelievers. Some scholars argue that in order to have rights a person must be a believer,[213] while respecting the secular so-called *universal* system is not incumbent on Muslims.

A second issue contributing to the traditional reluctance to deal with human rights is related to terminology. Some contemporary scholars have simply been unwilling to introduce what they consider to be the *new* terminology of rights and freedoms. Although it is undisputable that "the juristic discourse of the *fuqahā'* is conveyed[214] in a language which they felt was suitable to the prevailing conditions of their time,"[215] many continue to believe that the language of rights and freedoms is alien to Islam. The jurists argue that this is affirmed by the fact that "there are no categorical pronouncements in these sources [the Qur'an and Sunnah] which would identify fundamental rights as a separate category."[216] Such a claim, however, is not factual as the final part of this chapter demonstrates. Fundamental rights are identified in the Qur'an as *ḥudūd*, a concept that has been misunderstood and misused in traditional fiqh. The error, however, does not alter the word of God as it is expressed in the Qur'an. *ḥudūd* constitute the divinely ordained limits or boundaries of human behavior aimed at securing human rights in addition to those of other life forms.

Barring this serious inaccuracy, *maqāṣid* scholars among others have focused their attention on the openness of Islamic studies to new terminology. The late scholar and jurist Mahmood Ahmed Ghazi, for instance, argued that "terminologies of other traditions were [historically] accepted" in the Islamic tradition as a way to deal with new situations. Generally, scholars agree that "as long as a new concept resonates with Islamic principles, is consistent with our tradition, and does not conflict with our religious inheritance, we are correct in deeming it Islamic."[217] It is also reasonable to expect that different languages introduce different concepts that nevertheless comprise shared meanings.

The need for such rationalizations seem at odds with the position of Prophet Muhammad who had advised believers that "knowledge is the lost inheritance of the believer; wherever the believer finds it, he should take it."[218] This was confirmed by the fourth rightly guided caliph ʿAlī ibn Abī Ṭālib who exhorted Muslims to accept knowledge irrespective of the faith of the conveyor on the basis that its incorporation in the Muslim worldview would add important dimensions that may not have been part of its original discovery and articulation.[219] The issue of terminology appears to be quite superficial and has obscured attention from real concerns about the impact and substance of human rights for Islamic policy and governance.

The third factor that has sidetracked and indeed discouraged Muslim scholars from genuinely considering a theory of human rights in Islam has been their tendency to reject western liberal concepts of rights and associated freedoms. Many works disparage what are perceived to be the outcomes of unhindered rights and freedoms in secular states. Generally, the concept of freedom in western liberalism is viewed as a contributor to nationalism, capitalism and a generally lax attitude toward sexual morality. From this perspective, the absence of a spiritual compass that grounds humanity in a specific moral framework has accelerated social, political, economic and cultural decline.

The fourth and final concern of Islamic scholars with human rights and freedoms appears to be rooted in a reluctance to promote a social order that clearly defies the status quo in most predominantly Muslim countries and even within communities in secular states. The entrenchment of authoritarian dictatorships necessitates the violation of human rights, albeit to varying degrees. The presence or emergence of most traditional scholars in those parts of the world has led them to either steer clear of human rights issues or to support suppression in line with state orders. Unfortunately, some scholars welcome state repression to avoid an issue that they perceive carries heavy moral responsibility and where no clear guidance from traditional fiqh has been provided. Moreover, pressures within the religious establishment for members to conform to traditional opinions have stifled the promotion of rights and freedoms. Those who are outspoken are marginalized in religious councils and institutions while those who dare confront state authorities are reprimanded by more serious methods.

The Islamic discourse on human rights has therefore been undeniably timid. Generally, traditional scholars have not wished to be perceived as encouraging moral laxity, which is both a result of the limits of fiqh and *uṣūl al-fiqh* as well as a general lack of confidence in the conscience of the average believer. Some have also chosen to avoid the wrath of authoritarian regimes or disapproval of the more extreme members of their religious communities. This has not boded well for Islam's universalist claims, leading some to participate in the creation and endorsement of largely symbolic universal human rights instruments along the lines of the Universal Declaration of Human Rights of 1948 (UDHR). But the incapacity to offer a truly original contribution to the global discourse or an intrinsically appealing and religiously binding alternative for believers has significantly affected guidance for policy and governance. Thus far, Muslims have not produced an instrument anywhere near as popular as the UDHR, or more seriously, anything adequately reflective of the processes and content of the Shariʿah.

Islamic Human Rights Declarations

The determination of common ground between Islam and *universal* standards of human rights has for the most part been incorporated in the Islamic versions of the Universal Declaration of Human Rights. The two most important international documents, albeit non-binding, in this regard are the Universal Islamic Declaration of Human Rights (UIDHR) and the Cairo Declaration on Human Rights in Islam (CDHRI). The UIDHR was promulgated in 1981 by the London-based Islamic Council for Europe which is affiliated with the Muslim World League, an international NGO headquartered in Makkah, Saudi Arabia. The declaration is not an intergovernmental document but it was granted international status by UNESCO. In contrast, the CDHRI was promulgated in 1990 by the member states of the Organization of the Islamic Conference to provide an Islamic version of the UDHR. The main concerns of Muslim actors in both these developments was what they perceived as the incompatibility of an instrument largely based on secular tradition of the west and their interpretations of Divine law.

Similar to their secular counterparts, the Islamic versions include the rights to life, freedom, equality, justice, fair trial, protection against torture, asylum, as well as freedom of belief, speech, association, mobility, etc. In conformance to these broader understandings, a number of Muslim scholars actively assisted in the formulation and/or supported the ratification of the UIDHR and the CDHRI. The scholars affirmed that the Shariᶜah was the sole source of such attempts or as the reference for certain reservations regarding international human rights instruments. In light of this, some commentators praised these efforts because they served to attach Islamic authority to human rights giving them a stronger moral foundation for Muslims.[220]

Even thus, reference to the Shariᶜah in such general terms appears to be unjust for a number of reasons not the least of which is the ambiguity of what this means. The general tendency to refer to the Shariᶜah in these instruments has not been to preserve rights but to reserve leeway to restrict them. The reluctance to discuss rights without an immediate reference to constraints appears to be an integral part of these documents. In an explanatory note accompanying the English text, the UIDHR states: "each one of the Human Right enunciated in this declaration carries a corresponding duty." In addition, it also insists, "by the terms of our primeval covenant with God our duties and obligations have priority over our rights." This is seriously flawed since the main purpose of the duties and obligations alluded to *is* to guarantee the provision of rights, not to challenge, diminish or contradict them. Consequently, these efforts were accused of employing human rights instruments to disguise human rights abuses as well as compromising the *universal* consensus on which international human rights instruments were evolved.[221]

Indeed, Islamic contributions do not appear to have achieved the reputation of their secular counterparts or to have respected the nature, flexibility and dynamism of the Shariᶜah. Any instrument resulting from human efforts at a specific point in history responds to specific needs, fears and aspirations of the communities that created it. Imitating the UDHR or any other international human rights law by infusing it with fragmented Islamic concepts has not only been ineffective it has distracted stakeholders from developing genuine Islamic alternatives. In the cases of the UIDHR and the CDHRI, political pressures and religious bias in the production processes led to the inaccurate confinement of human rights in ways that do not reflect the richness of the Shariʿah and its responsiveness to human needs. This is ultimately reflected in their subsequent lack of credible authority.

Human Rights and the *Maqāṣid*

The *maqāṣid*, according to Auda, "represent the link between the Islamic law and today's notions of human rights, development and civility."[222] Indeed, the *maqāṣid* literature has dealt with rights and freedoms in four major ways. The first is very partial in that it takes the form of evolving the objectives of the preservation of religion and honor to either mean specific human rights or to include them. The outcome of these broader understandings has been expressed, as examined above, in documents such as the UIDHR and the CDHRI. A second stream argues that human rights form the foundation of significant Islamic principles that cannot be upheld if fundamental rights and freedoms are violated. This understanding insists that rights and freedoms, though not directly articulated in the texts, are nevertheless clearly implied in the principles and injunctions of the Shariʿah. A third stream, takes an interest-based approach to human rights by transforming all the *maqāṣid* into inalienable rights thereby incorporating all modern concepts into the traditional *maqāṣid* classification. Finally, a fourth stream argues that additional dimensions must be added to the essentials of *maqāṣid* including rights and freedoms. Each contribution is briefly discussed below.

Evolving the maqāṣid to mean or include human rights

The evolution of the objectives of the preservation of religion, as well as the preservation of honour, can most clearly be seen to accommodate human rights rhetoric. Thus, the preservation of religion has been "re-interpreted to mean a dramatically different concept, which is freedom of faith,' to use Ibn Ashur's words, or 'freedom of belief,' in other contemporary expressions."[223] The SIP asserts that the preservation of religion "prescribes the promotion of Islamic ethical values, freedom of religious choice, and the facilitation of religious practice to those who have made this choice."[224] Although this goes a long way toward distancing the preservation of religion from the mere question of belief or disbelief, it is far from reflecting the system of human rights and freedoms elaborated in the Qur'an.

Similarly, the preservation of honor "is gradually being replaced in the Islamic law literature with 'preservation of human dignity' and even the 'protection of human rights' as a purpose of Islamic law in its own right."[225] The SIP scholars have "broadened this *maqṣad* and have recognized human rights as intrinsic to the notion of human dignity and honour."[226] Rights and liberties are accorded to the people based on the principle of humanity. Rights that protect honor include "due process, protection from torture, arbitrary arrests and detention; protection of privacy (including privacy of the home and personal correspondence); protection from discrimination based on race, religion, and gender; and protection against public slander or libel."[227] More broadly, the SIP asserts that the preservation of honor involves the protection and furthering of human rights in general terms.

The challenge with this approach is that it seeks to re-interpret fiqh and sometimes the primary sources to demonstrate that human rights, as conventionally understood, are actually inherent to Islam. The Shariʿah, however, demonstrates that not all human rights that have been elaborated in secular systems are acceptable, while there are some rights in the Shariʿah that have yet to be acknowledged by secular standards. Second generation or social and economic rights, which are confirmed in the Shariʿah but remain contestable in secular systems, are a case in point.

Human rights as an indispensable basis of the maqāṣid

Freedom of expression has received significant attention in the Islamic discourse on human rights. Both the Qur'an and Sunnah recognize freedom of opinion in matters which have not been explicitly addressed in either texts though this is subject to moral and legal constraints, the violation of which is subject to punishment. The assumption of certain rights and freedoms as underlying key Qur'anic principles and injunctions is brilliantly explained in the award winning work of Mohammed Hashim Kamali (1998), *Freedom of Expression in Islam*.

Kamali argues that the objectives of freedom of expression are two-fold, namely, to reveal the truth and uphold human dignity.[228] One may add that freedom of expression is also critical for open and transparent communication so that we may know the positions and views of others, irrespective of perceptions of truth. Different forms of expression may not be our truths but they are the truths of others, and there is no way to communicate openly and honestly if people are not at liberty to express themselves. The Qur'an uses dialogue extensively to convey the details of historical events, and also to enact verbal exchanges that demonstrate freedom of expression and its etiquette. We can see in those exchanges that freedom of expression is not restrained in its content except to the extent that it remains free of personal attack and slander. Even the proclamation of disbelief is subject to reasoned argument and peaceful abandonment.

Kamali's basic thesis is that the principles of *ḥisbah* or commanding good and forbidding evil, *naṣīḥah* or sincere advice, *shūrā* or consultation, ijtihad or independent juristic reasoning, and *ḥaqq al-muʿāraḍah* or the right to opposition are rooted in and dependent upon freedom of expression, with freedom of association and assembly as associated dimensions. The author adopts Mahmassani's definition of freedom as "The ability of the individual to say or do what he or she wishes, or to avoid doing so, without violating the right of others, or the limits that are set by the law."[229] He also draws on the work of Bailey (1964) to add that freedom also means "the absence of restraints upon the ability of individuals or groups to communicate their ideas to others, subject to the understanding that they do not coerce others into paying attention or that they do not invade other rights essential to the dignity of the individual..."[230] By accepting these 'universal' definitions of freedom, Kamali is obliged to spend considerable effort delineating the limits that fiqh has placed on freedom.

Legal and moral constraints on freedom of expression are meant to contribute to the higher goal of maintaining a stable socio-political order, asserts Kamali. In other words, freedom of speech must remain deferential to the 'essential interests' (*maṣāliḥ ḍarūriyyah*). It is argued that the moral and legal restrictions on freedom of expression elaborated in the Qur'an and Sunnah address this overriding concern. Morally reprehensible expressions include backbiting, acrimonious talk, exposing the weaknesses of others, and certain types of lying. Legally prohibited behaviors include slander, libel, insult, sedition and blasphemy. The regulation of these potential abuses ensures that the exercise of freedom does not jeopardize the five essential values of life, faith, intellect, lineage and property.[231]

Defining an interest-based approach

Another distinguishable approach to human rights in the *maqāṣid* literature endorses a *maṣlaḥah* or interests based theory to human rights. According to Auda "there is resonance with advances in modern social research, which gives further evidence that the *Maqāṣid* theory seeks to fulfill fundamental human needs... it speaks to the basic needs of all human beings – needs and rights that must be protected."[232] From this perspective all six traditional *maqāṣid* are viewed as essential prerequisites for human wellbeing and as such justify claims to corresponding rights. In other words, all of mankind is entitled to the rights and freedoms that contribute to the preservation of religion, life, mind, progeny, wealth and dignity.[233] In this approach to human rights, the *maqāṣid* emerge as the inviolable beacons of humanity. People are permitted to live according to their traditions so long as they do not violate the *maqāṣid*, especially the right to life.[234] In this doctrine, people respect other people's rights because the *maqāṣid* are presented as Divine will.

The interest-based approach places special emphasis on the role of the state in protecting human rights and freedoms as largely understood in the secular sense. Two justifications are given for the perceived obligations of the state. *Ādamiyyah* or our inherent rights as the children of Adam forms the first justification. The second, is the acknowledgement that people need rights and freedoms in order for the state "*to create a fair testing environment*" or *ibtilā'*.[235] In this environment people are free to behave as they choose so long as an individual's actions "do not directly inflict harm on others."[236] In particular, the SIP scholars emphasize the importance of freedom of religion, conscience and rationality. They argue that any interference with these freedoms would result in "thwarting" God's purpose in creating humanity and would "interfere with the whole structure of the Muslim state."[237] It goes without saying, however, that no human power can *thwart* God's purpose. Moreover, the scholars make an unqualified stretch from a position of freedom of religion, conscience and rationality to the assertion that "it is not the role of the state to enforce a moral code."[238] In its essence the *maqāṣid is* a moral code, and particularly when it is presented as a foundation of policy or governance. In fact, the value-laden nature of policy and governance is widely accepted as a defining characteristic of the policy sciences. If not the *maqāṣid*, then some other moral code or combination of codes must rule.

Adding to the objectives of the maqāṣid

Perceiving of rights and freedoms as essentials is not new to the *maqāṣid* approach, if only marginal. Some prominent thinkers have proposed listing "justice, equality, freedom, and social, economic and political rights among the higher intents of the law", that is, as essentials.[239] Muhammad al-Ghazali has noted that, "there need to be additions to the five essentials of the Law... corrupt rule over the centuries has led to baneful outcomes. Hence, to the five essentials I would add freedom and justice... The five essentials might serve as criteria for [ruling on] secondary issues which we face; however, in order to regulate the order of the state, there has to be a guarantee of freedoms."[240] In a similar vein, al-Hasani observes:

> The identification of essential human interests in society is subject to what is dynamic in society and not to what is static, to what is variable and changing and not to what is constant or unchanging.... As such, it likewise calls for the recognition that these essentials include other interests as well, interests which Islamic society needs to preserve more at the present time: the right to free expression and freedom of political

> association, the right to elect and change our rulers, the right to employment, sufficient food, housing and clothing, the right to medical care, as well a long list of other rights which, like those mentioned here, are aptly considered to be essential to human existence in modern society.[241]

Recognition that rights must be added to the essential *maqāṣid* is a welcome development. The idea, however, that human rights are situated alongside other objectives like the preservation of religion rather than forming an intrinsic dimension of these objectives is at odds with the Shariʿah. The preservation of *Dīn* encompasses certain moral imperatives, including human rights, which cannot be compromised or considered as a separate dimension. Islam is something believers and non-believers alike experience through an unconditional expression of values, morals and ethical principles. These expressions are not equivalents or accessories to Islam, they are its very essence. Asked about what the *Dīn* is, the Prophet responded, *it is the beauty of ethical behavior*.[242] And in another narration, the Prophet says: "God has favored this religion for Himself and it is not suited for your religion except [to practice] generosity and the beauty of ethical behavior; indeed so adorn your religion with them."[243]

Rethinking the *Maqāṣid* Approach to Human Rights

The elaboration of a Qur'anic theory of human rights is beyond the scope of this chapter and perhaps beyond the capacity of this author. What I can glean from the Qur'an are a number of potentially guiding elements for a more comprehensive future project. The Qur'anic presentation of human rights addresses individuals, communities and governing authorities or more generally those with wealth and power. It sets standards for the most basic provisions on the individual level to more complex, overlapping and collective provision on the communal and state levels. For each unit from the individual to the nation, it establishes obligations, responsibility and sanction. The Qur'an seamlessly weaves human rights, and those of other creatures, into the very fabric of our humanity. Therefore, the diminution of a supply of ethical goods in its diverse manifestations is in essence a diminution of our humanity.

A clear and separate category within the Shariʿah

Human rights in Islam emanate from the Divine authority of the Qur'an. The knowledge available to elaborate an Islamic approach can partly be found in analyses that have already been performed, especially regarding morality in the Qur'an, and partly in the source texts which must be mined. But even before the initiation of this effort, policy analysts must reclaim a very important Qur'anic concept, namely, the *ḥudūd*. In traditional jurisprudence the *ḥudūd* have been defined as the body of corporal punishments articulated in the Qur'an and Sunnah. Understood as such, the *ḥudūd* "codify the limits on human behavior and prescribe physical punishment meted out for such misconduct. The six *ḥudūd* are murder, theft, taking up arms against the community of Muslims (treason), drunkenness, adultery, and slander (bearing false witness)."[244] This, however, is a juristic construct that does not respect the Qur'anic expression of the concept. In other words, "...the word *ḥudūd* is not used in the sense of mandatory fixed penalties in the Qur'an."[245]

In fact, the *ḥudūd* comprise the Shariʿah's clear articulation of a separate category for fundamental rights. A *ḥadd* (singular of *ḥudūd*) is a limit beyond which an individual or group violates Divine law and as such the balance of life. The *ḥudūd* are mentioned in nine Qur'anic verses. In every mention, it is evident that the concept is meant to promote human and especially women's rights. In four verses, the *ḥudūd* are mentioned in relation to the preservation of the rights of women during divorce where God commands believing men to be heedful of His *ḥudūd*, i.e., not to violate or in any way diminish the rights of women during times when the likelihood of committing injustices is heightened.[246] In the other instances, the *ḥudūd* are related to the rights of fasting and inheritance (*al-Baqarah*: 187; *al-Nisā'*: 13); inexcusability of lacking knowledge of *ḥudūd* (*al-Tawbah*: 97); and the consequences that those who transgress the *ḥudūd* should anticipate (*al-Nisā'*: 14). In *Sūrah al-Tawbah* the spirit of the word *ḥudūd* is most clear:

> (Triumphant) are those who turn repentant (to Allah), those who serve (Him), those who praise (Him), those who fast, those who bow down,

those who fall prostrate (in worship), those who enjoin the right and who forbid the wrong and those who keep the limits *ḥudūd* (ordained) of Allah - And give glad tidings to believers! (*Al-Tawbah*: 112)

We can see from the Qur'anic meaning of *ḥudūd*, that the concept is intricately associated with the likelihood that people are more prone to commit injustices when they are ignorant of the law, socially privileged, emotionally or physically distressed, or dealing with the distribution of wealth. It is precisely in these instances that the Qur'an reminds people of the fundamental and inviolable nature of human rights. As adverse circumstances are no excuse to violate the rights of others, it can be safely assumed that guarding such rights under normal circumstances is given. The *ḥudūd* establish the minimal standards beyond which individuals and larger social units commit injustice. In light of this, identifying, understanding and elaborating the implications of the *ḥudūd* for human welfare is an urgent project.

Human rights as ethical provisions

Generally, the Qur'anic conception of human rights can be understood as a *supply of ethical goods* based on an intricate system of social obligations. Whether in regard to individuals or larger social units the objective or *maqṣad* of the Qur'anic approach is to guarantee maximum provision with the *ḥudūd* establishing a minimum threshold. This is in stark contrast to the secular 'universal' approach that views human rights as *ethical demands* that are ultimately *satisfied* with minimal provision.

In the Qur'an, human rights are advanced as a supply of ethical goods, rooted in Divine command, and constitutive of a core element of faith. In other words, they are conceptualized as moral rules, which are primarily expressed as *legal* obligations. There is no pretension in this statement. The status of legislated rights by public authorities does not alter or compromise the binding nature of human rights for believers since moral and religious obligations and their implications extend beyond state prerogatives. Institutional force may bolster and standardize basic rights but it is not the decisive factor for believers whose aim is to heed the Divine. Their goal is not the adoption of minimal standards enforced (or not) by state authorities or in conformance with social custom but rather to strive to maximize the good they can do for others during their lifetimes. The Qur'an describes them as fulfilling their promises; feeding the needy, orphan and captive only for a love of God, wanting and expecting no reward or thanks, but rather protection from the distress of the Day of Judgment (*al-Insān*: 7-10). Through an appeal to their "intelligence, senses, tendencies, attractions, spiritual values, the inner light of conscience, the outer light of Revealed and non-revealed teaching"[247] the Qur'an brings these individuals to a recognition, an internalization, of Divine law. Institutionalization to them is not a condition or motivation to desist or act, they have internalized a higher law, one to which they know of a surety they will be held accountable.

Belief, and therefore the drive to provide human rights, is situated in the heart. The Qur'an states: "... it is not the sight that is blinded but rather blind are the hearts that are in the breasts" (*al-Ḥajj*: 46). Indeed, the potential harshness of the human heart may exceed the hardness of rocks, for as the Qur'an tells us, even among rocks are some from which water gushes forth, and others that split so that water can pass and yet others that plummet in awe of their Lord (*al-Baqarah*: 74). The heart and other human faculties play key roles in the provision of human rights (*al-Ḥajj*: 46).

The provision of human rights, however, is not completely personal. The Qur'an is replete with injunctions for communities and their governing authorities. Divine retribution is salient where human rights violations become rampant, i.e., where the *ḥudūd* are consistently and flagrantly ignored. The Qur'an recounts narratives of communities who were destroyed for their inequities. Pharaoh and his people were guilty of enslavement, manipulation and social division; Abraham's people were guilty of idol worship; Noah's people exhibited arrogance and class inequalities treating people in accordance with their wealth; the people of 'Ad were ostentatious, immoral and tyrannical; the people of Thamud were guilty of extravagance and denied the rights of nature; the people of Lot were guilty of sexual lewdness and public immorality; and, those of Shu'aib were guilty of commercial fraud and unfair trade practices.

These examples demonstrate something more than collective responsibility. They demonstrate the obligatory nature of what has come to be known as second generation rights in the contemporary secular literature. Although there is controversy in secular systems over whether second generation rights including social and economic rights constitute human rights, largely because of the challenge of institutionalization, the Qur'an makes clear that these are legitimate rights irrespective of the human will to support them. Environmental, cultural, social, political and economic rights are a collective responsibility, which demand adequate provision and public attention. The Qur'an consistently reiterates that a dignified existence cannot be actualized in the absence of these rights.

Dignity as the guiding principle

Unlike the secular human rights model which posits freedom as the most important value, the message of Islam emphasizes the importance of human dignity, which accepts freedom as a necessary but insufficient contributor to human rights. Dignity is defined as the "quality of being worthy of honour or respect."[248] The Qur'an states: "We dignified the children of Adam and carried them in the land and the sea; and granted them from all that is good and fair; and preferred them over much of what we created with notable preference" (*al-Isrā'*: 70). *Al-ādamiyyah* or the concept that we are all the children of Adam entitles us all to *ḥuqūq al-ādamiyyīn* or the rights of humans.[249] Ibn Ashur among others had asserted that human beings are equal with respect to their essentials and needs. He argued that the inborn constitution (*takwīn)* "means that the very existence of human beings is the basis of certain inalienable rights that are linked to them in their creation."[250]

The Qur'an makes amply clear that *everyone* has the right to a happy, peaceful life. Let everyone eat and enjoy is an expression used in a number of verses (*al-Mursalāt*: 46, *Yā Sīn*: 35). Those who desire the transitory bounties of this life are given it (*al-Isrā'*: 18). Believers are given no recourse against people who do not fight them (*al-Nisā'*: 90) and they are not permitted to 'make haste against them'.[251] This also applies to believers who take their religion for play and distraction (*al-Anʿām*: 70) for whom only reminders are permitted (*al-Anʿām*: 70; *al-Naḥl*: 82). These commands reinforce the universality of human rights in Islam, which are clearly not contingent on the characteristics of the recipient.

The believer must recognize that what he or she provides is ultimately for him or herself. It is the believer that is in need to give, to supply those goods that will ultimately determine his or her fate and nearness to God. The believer accepts that the provision of human rights establishes their relationship with God.

> Behold God will say on the Day of Resurrection: "O children of Adam! I was ill and you did not comfort Me." The person will exclaim: "O Lord, how could I have comforted you, the Lord of all worlds?" And God will reply did you not know that such and such of my servants was ill, and you did not comfort him? Did you know that if you had done so, you would have indeed found Me with them? O children of Adam! I asked for food, but you did not feed Me." The person will exclaim: "O Lord, how could I have fed you, the Lord of all worlds?" God will say: "Did you not now that such and such of my servants asked you for food, and you did not feed him? Did you not know that if you had done so, you would have found it with Me? O children of Adam! I asked you for a drink, but you did not give me to drink." The person will say: "How could I have given you, the Lord of the worlds to drink?" But God will reply: "Such and such of my servants asked you for a drink, but you did not give it to him. Did you not know that if you had given it to him to drink you would have found it with Me?"[252]

In short, God is the ultimate recipient of these goods and so their quantity and quality should always be at their best. This approach mitigates human tendency to let emotions, discrimination and otherwise avoidable excuses impact the supply of ethical goods. It also upholds the dignity of the recipient who, irrespective of circumstance, actually privileges the provider with his acceptance.

From an Islamic perspective dignity is the most suitable human condition. It entails mutual respect, honor, giving, love, care, compassion and service to others. Although most people appreciate the provision of a wide scope of life choices or freedoms, human dignity precedes, envelops and constrains this state. To dignify others is to ensure that they are living at their best and that the bearers of obligation are fulfilling the God-given rights of all creation. Human rights cannot merely be an instrument for people to seek protection from each other's violence or to motivate some to act on the behalf of others as they have come to be commonly conceived. Dignity cannot be fully actualized through freedom alone. In fact, freedom is often curtailed to protect human dignity.

Among the benefits of centralizing dignity is to ensure that real differences among us do not impair the qualities of our lives. The Qur'an affirms that some people are raised above others in ranks so that we may be able to commission each other in various ways (*al-Zukhruf*: 32). This is a very serious reality when we are examining the importance of the dignity of human beings in our formulation of human rights. The blessing of being able to employ and benefit from this diverse and unequal distribution of resources and talents carries great responsibility and is not to be taken lightly. To insist that all human beings are equally capable of impacting each other is fictitious. By acknowledging this reality, the Qur'an establishes rules to ensure that people do not mistreat each other on account of a Divine law that is intended only to facilitate life. Those who are at an advantage are not *free* to do as they please. Irrespective of their advantages and power, they are commanded to dignify others who may not be so generously endowed. This ensures that if the supply of rights owed to people were to adjust on account of their psychological, physical, material or even moral differences it can only be to improve their condition.

Obligations and Duties

Human rights generate a justification for action on the part of every believer to safeguard the dignity of others with whom they either have an immediate affinity or toward whom they have a duty to support by virtue of their knowledge, capacity and resources. The nature of support ranges from actions as simple as a smile to much greater efforts involving one's time, wealth, and in the most extreme case, life. The Prophet stated: "The doors of goodness are many...enjoining good, forbidding evil, removing harm from the road, listening to the deaf, leading the blind, guiding one to the object of his need, hastening with the strength of one's legs to one in sorrow who is asking for help, and supporting the feeble with the strength of one's arms–all of these are charity prescribed for you." He also said: "Your smile for your brother [broadly defined] is charity."[253] These actions comprise a main pillar in a believer's moral world and understanding of faith.

The rules pertaining to human rights in the Qur'an, just as those pertaining more generally to morality, are both fixed and flexible. "Because of its clarity, the tenor of each rule erects a kind of barrier against disorder and anarchical fancy; but through its indetermination, it allows individuals to choose the form by which they must adapt their ideal to the conditions of existence and conciliate their present duty with all other requirements of morality."[254] Human rights, being a subset of the Qur'an's moral rules, also reflect this characterization. Within the believer, just as within larger social units, there ought to be a continuous calibration of what and how to provide human rights.

The mutability of rights, beyond the *ḥudūd*, is a result of the pragmatic nature of Islamic morality. Rights subject to personal choice cover all the decisions that we can potentially make in our daily lives that impact others. In this category only the individual and God know the extent of possible supply. Duties in the Qur'an are not elaborated with quantitative or qualitative details. Draz argues that this is the case "in order to be entrusted to the opinion of the ordinary conscience, but also every Qur'anic obligation posits a number of considerations as a condition for its application, which makes it necessary simultaneously to take into account the human potential, the concrete circumstances and the harmony of our duties."[255] In other words, the provider of rights knows how much time, energy and wealth they can expend to help a homeless person to buy a meal or find shelter. Every provider, whether individual or group, has a choice at a specific moment to give or withhold resources or talents. Qur'anic obligation "grants every individual conscience some part in the legislative action, a part which is necessary for formulating one's concrete duty at every moment."[256] Some individuals and groups will excel in providing such goodness, others will follow a middle course, and yet others will wrong their souls (*Yā Sīn*: 32). To each is his account and reward. People who have good fortune in this life have a greater responsibility to be just and generous (*al-Nūr*: 22).

Rights subject to public scrutiny and decision-making are those that necessarily depend on collective capacities and public authority to deliver. Communities are morally responsible although ultimate judgment is a personal affair. In this life, communities and nations make collective decisions in some form or another that impact the lives of their members in addition to those beyond their borders. The Qur'an is clear in its warning against the neglect of injustices that are to the detriment of all. Communities *owe* their members certain rights based on their endowments, capacities, resources and aspirations.

Shūrā or collective decision-making takes on special significance in the public sphere. The ambiguity in the methods and quantity of the vast substance of rights provisions demands ongoing assessment of resources, capabilities and alternatives for realizing the optimal social balance. Public engagement and agreement is indispensable throughout this process of deliberation, the nature and outcomes of which are no less obligatory than those emanating from individual determinations. The flexibility of the Shariʿah in this regard means that rights, with exception to the *ḥudūd* or what is considered very basic, are always changing, open to dispute, and necessarily based on communal will or political exigencies. This dynamism is intended to encourage social units to reflect upon, identify, and practice human rights in ways that conform to the advancement of knowledge and sensibilities as well as the prevailing context and capacities, always aspiring for what satisfies *maqāṣid al-sharīʿah* at that particular moment.

The path to supplying human rights

Unlike the secular human rights model, where legislation emerges as the pre-eminent and decisive factor in practice, an Islamic approach is based on the moral imperatives of belief including the surety of accountability before God, both in this life and the next. The establishment of a law that can be applied individually to every conscience is only possible within a religious system that accepts the omnipotence of God, and His uninhibited ability to judge every person in proportion to the bounties with which He has granted them during their lifetime. Thus, the Qur'an has a clear inclination toward situating human rights in a supply-oriented framework. Prophet Muhammad said: "Whosoever of you sees an evil, let him change it with his hand; and if he is not able to do so then with his tongue [through communication]; and if he is not able to do so then with is heart [through silent prayer] – and that is the weakest of faith."[257]

The duties that believers commit to undertake clearly impact the provision of the rights of others. A commitment to any duty is rooted in the religious concept of *taqwā* variously translated as piety, fear of God, or God consciousness, though a preferable understanding is most closely related to *heedfulness*. To heed is to remain aware of or pay close attention to something. God states that the *most dignified* among people are the *most heedful* (*al-Ḥujurāt*: 13). The Islamic doctrine of human rights does not simply aim at "identifying fundamental prerequisites for each human being to live a minimally good life"[258] but rather presents an internal and external reality that aims at guaranteeing the believer and everyone around him or her a maximally good life. *Taqwā* encompasses our continuous struggle to ensure that our inner beings and our external manifestations maximize the provision of ethical goods for ourselves and for others throughout our lives. As Draz explains, "on the road from the ordinary duty to the perfect duty, which is offered to each person's initiative and courage the Qur'an marks each step by its degree of merit, and while showering the various progressive applications of virtue with its beneficence, it invites those of its supporters always to climb higher."[259] This is the engine of Islam's dynamism as it applies to the supply of human rights.

To be heedful is to continuously and consistently express *taqwā*. The greater one's *taqwā*, the greater will be the quantity and quality of the ethical goods that one supplies at any given moment. As our natural and attained knowledge, capacities and resources change during our lifetimes we are always open to improving the manifestations of our *taqwā* by increasing and refining our duties. Heedfulness entails provision or supply even when there is no overt demand. It is to understand that demand is not the critical factor which motivates *taqwā* but rather the desire, indeed the need, to supply ethical goods. *Taqwā* is the tool by which believers fulfill their covenant with God.

Taqwā is both a personal and social phenomenon. In the personal realm, as implied above, *taqwā* is situated within the heart. Prophet Muhammad said: "Heedfulness is here" and he pointed to his heart three times.[260] Its positioning in the heart extends from that organ's infinite capacity to do good based on its potential power to illuminate, sensitize and foresee. God enhances the strength of believers' hearts in order that they may grasp the true meaning and implications of heedfulness (*al-Ḥujurāt*: 3). Indeed, a genuine commitment to the complete implications of *taqwā* requires intense tranquility and complete trust in God (*al-Fatḥ*: 26), a state that believers strive toward but rarely fully achieve. When *taqwā* diminishes so too does the supply of ethical goods.

Withholding an ethical good on an individual basis tends to be socially acceptable when it does not fall below a minimum threshold or when others have no way of knowing of the violation. The latter often occurs when, based on knowledge, capacity and resources, provision is morally expected to exceed minimum thresholds but does not do so due to individual or group power, authority, secrecy, protection, etc. As this decline in the provision of human rights gradually becomes widespread within a society it makes way for more noticeable violations. Because of its gradualism, bolstered by the acquiescence of society, an injustice can become a social phenomenon that has the endorsement of socially dominant groups.

In a series of narratives, the Qur'an conveys the social implications of the absence of *taqwā* among several ancient communities. The major injustice prevalent within each community represents a grave and timeless violation of human rights as described earlier. The direct connection of injustice to the concept of *taqwā* is evident as different messengers sent to each community ask the same question of their people, *will you not heed,* with each making the same demand of their people, *so heed God and obey me*. In each case the neglect of *taqwā* results in such rampant oppression that the ability to undertake good and right either implicitly or explicitly becomes impossible, while rectifying the social order no longer depends on individual and isolated reform but requires the concerted will of the people and potentially Divine intervention.

The rules for our communal lives, are not much different from those elaborated for our individual and personal endeavors. All rules contain a double imperative: a duty and a duty of perfection.[261] "All our social institutions must include a static, conservative part, which is to be protected from the caprice of human beings and circumstances, and a dynamic, evolutionary liberal part. From this we will be able to achieve our dreams of *stability* and *change*, our needs for *order* and *progress*," asserts Draz.[262] The Qur'an establishes clear moral grounds that the vast majority of community members can adhere to but then provides for and encourages the highest aspirations.

Taqwā both underlies and goes beyond conventional domains of action. Human rights law, advocacy, and public recognition are all important domains of action but they are only manifestations of effort not its source. Islam focuses on addressing the source of human rights and how we can achieve them. Prophet Muhammad had said: "No one has real faith unless he desires for his brother [brethren] that which he desires for himself." [263] The quantity and quality of ethical goods that we supply reflect the extent of our *taqwā* and the depth of our faith.

> Faith, in turn, takes its value from being the privilege of humble, sensitive hearts ... To open one's ears to its warnings is therefore the first manifestation of life, but to live it out, as it was by the Prophet, is moral greatness. Best of all, to practice it with others is to build a community into the best nation of the world.[264]

This brings us to the final topic of this chapter, namely, universality. Indeed, it would be natural to question the universality of a religious approach to human rights. For all the appeal of the Qur'an to human reason and the almost complete absence of acts of worship from the approach elaborated above, this discussion is without doubt rooted in Islam.

Universality as a condition of faith

This doctrine is based on a religious ethics and should be no more contestable on those grounds than one based on secularism. Even secularism must derive its morality from some source. A believer understands that morality demands "... resort to a higher authority which can decide the matter; [and that] it is certainly not in *society* that one can find this authority."[265] The secular model's denial or suppression of Divine authority and as such the entire edifice of moral obligation that corresponds to it, has rendered human rights of much less potency than should and must be the case. The primary act of faith for the believer "implies an acknowledgment that God is worthy to be obeyed, as well as loved and adored,"[266] which has wide ranging implications for everything that He created and granted us custodianship over. Why should the godless be considered the universal standard, a discourse in which it is insisted everyone can participate? The viability of any human rights approach should rest in its effectiveness, i.e., what it actually achieves for humanity and whether its postulates can amount to anything more than rhetoric.

The inescapable aspect of universality in the Qur'anic approach to human rights lies in the unconditional provision of rights to every human being. In this regard it clearly states: "O you who believe, stand out firmly for God, as fair witnesses and do not let hatred of others make you swerve from justice. Be just, it is closest to heedfulness and be heedful of God for God is well acquainted with what you do" (*al-Mā'idah*: 8). Therefore, accepting Islam may be necessary on the supply side of this human rights approach, but it is certainly not required on the receiving end. There is absolutely no verse in the Qur'an or credible narration in the Sunnah that limits the provision of what is good and ethical to Muslims only. Indeed, freedom to believe is a fundamental tenet of Islam and is not a condition for the provision of rights. God says whoever wills may believe and whoever wills may disbelieve (*al-Kahf*: 29). This life is given in its full glory to all of God's creation. Believers are commanded to be patient and good in their treatment of everyone (*al-Muzzammil*: 10).

The moral framework in the Qur'an provides clear and practical standards for the universal provision of human rights, while granting broad latitude for individuals and larger social groups to excel in the ways of doing so.

It is God who ultimately receives our provision of ethical goods, including human rights, if it is indeed toward Him that we truly dedicate our service. If we compete with others in this life, it can only be to do good, to perfect our duties with generosity and beauty. The Qur'an is a guide and a warning to believers. Our ability to tap its resources rests on our heedfulness of its message and the spirit of its guidance. As Draz concludes, "... if we search through this system for one central idea, one fundamental virtue, in which all commandments are condensed, we will find it is the notion of *taqwā*, or piety... to have the deepest respect for the law."[267] If that renders the application of the approach relevant for believers only, then so be it.

Conclusion

Perhaps one of the most critical concepts in any discussion of governance is human rights. The historical lack of an indigenous approach that is well developed, situated and respected within Islamic scholarship and Muslim practice has had serious implications for governance at all social levels. This, despite the fact that the Qur'an provides a comprehensive and powerful moral system within which human rights are centrally positioned.

This chapter concerned itself with exploring how Islamic scholarship has dealt with the topic of human rights. It suggested four primary reasons for the hesitation observed on the part of Islamic scholars to deal comprehensively with this topic. These relate to difficulties in reconciling the Divine source of the Shariʿah with the human source of secular human rights standards including the status of the disbeliever. The issue of alien terminology also creates disagreement among scholars who have traditionally been hesitant to incorporate non-native concepts in their works. This is reinforced by a general disdain for western liberalism and in particular perceptions that human rights and freedoms contribute to lax morality. Finally, there appears to be reluctance in the promotion of a full-fledged human rights agenda due to political but also religious pressures rooted in a long and complex legal heritage.

The chapter also explored how human rights have been advanced in the *maqāṣid* literature. Here human rights are integrated through (1) an evolution of the *maqāṣid* to incorporate modern human rights, (2) positing human rights as the foundation of key Islamic concepts, (3) transforming the *maqāṣid* themselves into inalienable rights, and (4) simply adding rights and freedoms alongside the other higher objectives of the Shariʿah. Though these contributions present important insights, they do not establish human rights with the force evident in the Qur'an's moral system.

The Qur'an presents an ethical system to which hundreds of millions of people subscribe. There is no Muslim of an intelligent and healthy disposition who would disagree with the duties enumerated in the Qur'an and further explained in the Sunnah, irrespective of their ability or willingness to practice. The discussion here has sought to relate the moral theory in the Qur'an to an Islamic approach to human rights. Its main contributions are its reclamation of the concept of *ḥudūd* as the minimum and inviolable standards of the Shariʿah as well as an emphasis on a supply orientation and hence maximization of human rights. All social units from the individual to the nation have essential duties beyond which duties do not cease to be obligatory but rather become contingent on prevailing conditions.

The religious basis of this approach may lead to a *lack of universality* critique. However, there is no reason why a godless system would be any less controversial or any more acceptable. In the final analysis the hope is to reach an understanding that believers can accept and recognize as their own. The stipulation that belief is only necessary on the supply side of the human rights equation should ease any apprehension. If Islam obligates believers to provide full rights to others without discrimination, there should be limited if any objection. From the perspective of the Shariʿah, universality is found in the unquestioning provision of ethical goods to all creation irrespective of demand.

6

Ethics of Governance and Public Policy in Islam

Verily God sends to this Ummah at the head of every one hundred years someone who will renew the *Dīn* for it.

PROPHET MUHAMMAD[268]

When one considers the most common advice dispensed to governments aiming to display an *Islamic* façade, one would be forgiven for believing that the Shariʿah is the furthest source of mercy and justice. The late scholar and jurist Mahmood Ahmed Ghazi explained that as the dictators of the 20th Century invited scholars to advise them, "these scholars simply formulated a penal code from *ḥudūd* [corporal punishments]... conveniently ignoring social justice, equality, simplicity and enhancement of the common man's lot."[269] The infusion of an *Islamic* contribution to governance almost always entails measures that conjure images of violence and injustice. The views of *maqāṣid* scholars are rarely acknowledged let alone solicited for policy input. This helps to explain serious concerns that are often expressed in environments where there is a credible possibility of introducing Islamic policy ideas. Given this reality, a return to the ethics of governance and public policy elaborated in the primary sources cannot be overstated.

In its essence, the *maqāṣid* approach involves an identification and application of the ethical principles articulated or implied within the Shariʿah. For classical jurists the six essential *maqāṣid* including the preservation of religion, life, dignity, mind, progeny and wealth encompasses all the benefits intended by Islamic law. Conversely, any action that jeopardizes these objectives are classified as harms. Some scholars have also presented suggestions concerning the determination of harms and benefits though these in no way constitute precise calculations. Moreover, the ethical parameters of such contributions are usually confined to Muslims, and even then to Muslims within a specific geographic location. In other words, the question of who is counted in these accounts of harms and benefits is very limited and not reflective of the Shariʿah. Is humanity or a portion of it the sole focus or are other creatures included? This chapter is not intended to offer solutions but rather to highlight the fundamental ethical philosophy and expanse of the Shariʿah. It is a foundational discussion for studies in public policy and governance in Islam, since its conclusions must necessarily guide the determination of benefits and harms.

The chapter is divided into four parts. The first part examines the philosophy of *tawḥīd* demonstrating the intricate relationship among all creation and among creation and the Creator. The second part then examines how *maqāṣid* scholars have dealt with the issue of benefits and harms. The concept of ummah constitutes the focus of part three as this is the most common reference for many Islamic scholars when discussing benefits and harms. I explain that contrary to popular understanding, the concept of ummah has broad application and is not limited to humans. Given our knowledge of the Shariʿah and its emphases, the fourth part suggests that the ethics of public policy and governance in Islam must necessarily go beyond the anthropocentrism that has characterized the better part of Islamic jurisprudence to date.

Tawḥīd

The beginning of wisdom in this discussion of ethics is the philosophical principle of *tawḥīd* or unification. *Tawḥīd* is the core principle in the Shariʿah's philosophy. The Qur'anic injunction not to sever what must be joined (*al-Baqarah*: 27; *al-Raʿd*: 25) is expressive of the complexity, depth and breadth of *tawḥīd*. It is this moral principle that presents governance and policy with a dilemma that can only be resolved through the practical ethics presented in the primary sources, which must be mined and articulated by the faithful scholars of every era who necessarily have a solid grounding in the Revealed and unrevealed word.

Al-tawḥīd or unification represents the heart of the Shariʿah's moral philosophy. The most profound admission that every believer must accept is that God is the one and only deity. This testimony is at one and the same time uniquely simple and infinitely complex. Its simplicity lies in its factual truth. There is no God but God. The Qur'an tells us that there is nothing like Him (*al-Ikhlāṣ*: 4). In its most accessible understanding, *tawḥīd* refers to belief in the oneness of God. At a more complex and sophisticated level of understanding, *tawḥīd* demands the translation of this philosophy into a way of life that integrates the Revealed and unrevealed word of God as if to read one book (*kitāb*). In the words of al-Faruqi, "*al-tawḥīd* is a general view of reality, of truth, of the world, of space, of time, of human history and destiny."[270] It is clear then that *tawḥīd* can only be understood and realized to the extent of our capacity to perceive and experience the universe's infinite diversity as an interconnected whole both in time and space. This reality is variously alluded to in the Qur'an. Thus, understanding *tawḥīd* with any depth demands a strong grasp of the content of the Qur'an and its references to the universe.

For believers, reality is comprised of God and non-God or Creator and created. Similarly, the Qur'an is the Word of God while all else including fiqh belongs in the realm of creation. In other words, reality includes two orders identified by al-Faruqi as the *duality principle*.[271] In the first order, which I term the supreme order, God is unique, with no partners. Al-Faruqi suggests that our relation to the supreme order is based on the *ideational principle*, that is, "memory, imagination, reasoning, observation, intuition, apprehension, etc."[272] The work of Draz demonstrates that through the vehicle of morality the believer's relationship is potentially much deeper than this. He suggests that these capacities may be employed to assimilate and synthesize sacred law in a way that dignifies human nature and allows each individual to partake in the development and expression of the law, a process I refer to as the *fusion principle*. In doing so we are not merely collaborating with the supreme order, we are essentially fusing with it. Draz explains:

> True morality is neither pure *submission*, nor absolute *invention*; it is *both together*. It is not the attitude of a *slave* or of an absolute *master*,

> but that of a *citizen*, participating in some way in the authority of the law, by the choice and initiative which are his rights... On the one hand, by adhering to sacred law, our *conscience* assimilates it, upholds it, makes it its *own*, as if it participated in the creation of eternal truths. On the other hand, when we synthesise different established rules, adjusting them to our situation, we do not do so in the absence of a master, but under his patronage, his *care* and *control*. We are always inspired by him, as if he still continues within us his role as legislator, down to the minutest detail. From this one can say that here, between the agent and author of the law, there is not only *collaboration*, but *union*. One could say a fusion of two wills.[273]

Islam thus renders the duality between God and believer a function of the believer's effort. As the teachings of the Qur'an are internalized, they gradually become part of our inner being, providing us with the guidance we need to make ethical choices and enabling us to move beyond the literal word into the infinite meanings of its combination with the world. The ultimate outcome of this process is unification, *tawḥīd*, of our will with the will of God.

The second order, or the realm of non-God, encompasses more than humanity. It includes "all creatures, the world of things, plants, animals, humans jinn and angels, heaven and earth, paradise and hell, and all their becoming since they came into being."[274] The second order must further be classified into two sub-orders. The first sub-order is comprised of each human being, a unique purposeful individual. Every human being in the second order is incomparable to every other and as such is irreplaceable by any other once he or she has come into being. Everything beyond the individual comprises the second sub-order. The relationship of each individual (first sub-order in second order) and how they act upon all other elements in the second order (second sub-order of second order) reflects the extent of his or her *fusion* with the supreme order.

Every individual, along with all created matter, is a purposeful point in the vastness of both the seen and unseen. The principle of teleology in the philosophy of *tawḥīd* states that the nature of the cosmos is purposive out of design.[275] This is a fundamental precept of the *maqāṣid* approach. The Qur'an innumerably draws our attention to Divine design. People who contemplate the magnificence of life cannot help but observe that it is the truth, an orderly, purposeful reality (*Āl ʿImrān*: 191). In addition to being challenged to contemplate God's perfection of the universe (*al-Mulk*: 3-4), we are explicitly informed of such perfection, measure and balance.[276] Human beings are capable of discerning the Divine laws or *sunnan* by which the intricacies of the universe are ordered in accordance with their individual capacities. Indeed, our physical and psychic functions are also subject to such determinations though our spiritual function is not. "Human action is the only instance where the will of God is actualized not necessarily, but deliberately, freely, voluntarily."[277]

The teleology principle demands that each unique individual discover their life's purposes. The Qur'an confirms that each person has a disposition or goal to which he or she tends and thus it exhorts us to use whatever inborn or acquired talents, capacities, and skills to race to do good works (*al-Baqarah*: 148). Humans are commanded and expected to capitalize on their diversity to achieve greatness and unity. The differences in our dispositions or tendencies endow humanity with strength and resilience so long as there is mutual respect. This applies at the group level as well, where the Qur'an tells us that different communities exhibit distinctive ways of life that God has facilitated for them and from them; correspondingly, each is given the attendant means to achieve their goals (*al-Mā'idah*: 48). Communities, just like individuals, are commanded to excel in doing good (*al-Mā'idah*: 48).

Though the complexity and magnitude of creation may render each person infinitesimally small, the fact that each individual comes to exist makes their presence eternal. For believers, the issue is how we wish to exist in this inevitably transitory phase and more significantly in the next eternal and final destination. Accepting *tawḥīd* commits believers to *ethical action*. Each individual's concern with their ultimate destination is the motivation to supply the maximum quantity and quality of ethical goods in this transitory phase. In other words, attaining the best of what is yet to come is contingent on supplying one's best in the here and now.

From this perspective, a lifespan is perceived as the physical distance between an individual and God and the Shariʿah is accepted as the navigation guide to achieve nearness to Him. The Qur'an is an indispensable tool in attaining this understanding. No extent of purely worldly understanding can replace the guidance of the Qur'an while no extent of Qur'anic knowledge in isolation of the world of observation to which it is inextricably linked can likewise suffice. Human understanding is not strong enough to appreciate God's will without understanding the diverse forms of its expression both Revealed and unrevealed. Understanding necessarily remains incomplete when attention to one or the other is neglected.

Thus, our relation to everything in the second order is both ideational and concrete in nature. Any translation of moral imperatives into action necessarily involves physical and/or material elements. This engagement between the self and second order is a reflection of how each person practices their faith. It is based not only on the extent of each's knowledge of the second order but more importantly on the willingness to supply it with ethical goods using each's unique synthesis of established rules adjusted to the specificities of existing conditions.[278]

The second order is therefore inextricably linked in moral, physical and material ways. On the axiological level *al-tawḥīd* presents one fundamental meaning, namely that all creation is in one way or another joined and hence dependent. Humans do not come into being without the primordial instinct to attachment. God says that he created us from *ʿalaq* or a thing that attaches or clings (*al-ʿAlaq*: 2). In nature dependence is manifested in infinite expressions. In affirmation, God's command to read or recite is done so in the name of *He who created.* From the very first verse of Revelation, the inseparability of the word and world is established.

Divine law dictates that life is inextricably linked, mutually reinforcing and dependent in a delicately determined balance. People are commanded not to sever what God has commanded to be joined (*al-Raʿd*: 25; *al-Baqarah*: 27). The profoundness of this command is very difficult to contemplate since the ability to see that all created matter is related in one way or another is limited by the current state of knowledge. In an incredibly profound verse, the Qur'an draws our attention to the significance of a gnat and all that is above it (*al-Baqarah*: 26). The Qur'an states that only those who reject faith cannot see the point of the illustration. Their description in the following verse as those who break their covenant with God after it has been ratified and separate or literally cut-off what God has ordered to be joined and corrupt the earth, is key to understanding the significance of the reference to the gnat and all that is above it. Only those with a deep understanding of *tawḥīd,* identified in the Qur'an as *'ulū al-albāb* (*al-Raʿd*: 19) or those who possess the light of unification, of deep comprehension and intellect, recognize the truth of the matter. They are the ones who accept and defend the moral imperative to guard an order that not only holds all life sacred but that also conserves, protects and promotes the linkages upon which life is necessarily dependent. This understanding and the attendant actions to unite what God has ordered be united is obligatory for believers (*al-Raʿd*: 21). The command to acknowledge the role and place of a gnat in the earthly web of life serves to draw attention to the higher significance of humans and their relations. How much more is the responsibility to understand and uphold the intricacies of our purposeful existence?

Undoubtedly, it is very challenging if at all possible to compass the extent, complexity and interdependence of all creation let alone the linkages among them. What we lack in knowledge, however, must yield to faith and the principles that were established by Divine providence to enable human beings to minimize harm. Even if we cannot predict the potential implications of necessary actions in advance, we must avoid self-deception and recognize the signs of corruption when they become evident (*al-Baqarah*: 11, 27). The excuse that 'this is the way things have always been' or 'the way we inherited from our fathers' or 'the way God intended,' is not acceptable for God does not command anything harmful or indecent (*al-Aʿrāf*: 28).

The question then naturally arises as to what the principle and practice of *tawḥīd* means for policy and governance in Islam. At the outset let us establish what it does not mean. It does not mean a global caliphate. There is absolutely no mention, explicit or implied, in the Qur'an, Sunnah, or early Islamic rule, to support this phenomenal claim. One of the essential objectives of *tawḥīd* is actually a recognition and respect for the diversity that makes up this unified and purposeful whole. This is no less true of the governance systems that color and shape the lives of distinct political units around the world. The right to self-determination is firmly established in the Qur'an for religious communities (5:42-48) and for political entities (*al-Naml*: 23-44). Accepting *tawḥīd* means recognizing its implications for decision-making at different levels of governance. Whether at the level of individuals, communities, nations or supranational organizations, *tawḥīd* introduces a philosophy that insists on the harmony of all living creatures and that situates human beings among, not above, other creation.

The Determination of Benefits and Harms

The determination of benefits and harms within the traditional *maqāṣid* literature occupies an important position. In fact, traditional scholars have generally presented the application of *maqāṣid* as an achievement of benefits and/or a prevention of harms.[279] Al-Ghazali had asserted that whatever promotes the preservation of the five essentials is a benefit and whatever threatens them is a harm.[280] According to al-ʿIzz ibn ʿAbd al-Salām "the benefits to be found in this world include everything termed 'essentials' or 'needs' under Islamic law, or by their complements and auxiliaries... and as for this world's sources of harm, they include the occurrence of whatever is contrary to the afore mentioned."[281] "In the end," Auda observes, the *maqāṣid* are "...for the *maṣlaḥah* [best interests] of the people, for enabling people to live a good life, that is, a good Islamic life according to Islamic criteria."[282]

In order to achieve benefits, decisions must be made in such a way that accounts for and promotes the preservation of religion, life, mind, progeny, wealth and dignity. These six objectives are synonymous with the public interest and their pursuit through various approaches and instruments is called *siyāsah sharʿiyyah* or Shariʿah-oriented politics. For the classic scholars like Ibn Qayyim al-Jawziyyah (d.1350 CE), *siyāsah sharʿiyyah* includes "any measure which brings the people closest to beneficence (*ṣalāḥ*) and furthest away from corruption (*fasād*) partakes in just *siyāsah* even if it has not been approved by the Prophet, nor regulated by Divine Revelation."[283]

In actual practice the final determination of benefits (*maṣāliḥ*) and harms (*mafāsid*) are very complex. It is rare to find purely beneficial solutions (*nafʿ khāliṣ*) to a public problem just as it is rare to implement purely harmful alternatives (*ḍurr khāliṣ*). Though these extremes may exist, most policy alternatives lie somewhere in between. Most governance matters are not amenable to a clear distinction between benefits and harms. Al-Shāṭibī drew on the concept of preponderance to support the determination of benefits and harms. According to this concept, the benefit must predominate the harm for a decision to be beneficial. If, in contrast, a harm predominates, then the decision is deemed harmful.[284] How to determine the balance that tips the scales in favor of either a harm or a benefit, however, is not clear. Indeed, Ibn Ashur asserted that his processors had failed to articulate suitable criteria for identifying an action as a benefit or harm.

In his *Treatise on Maqāṣid al-Sharīʿah*, Ibn Ashur proposed five criteria for identifying and weighing the benefits and harms of actions. First, the benefit or harm must be definite and regular. Second, the benefit or harm must be of a nature that is easily recognizable by reasonable individuals. Third, the characteristics of the action must render it irreplaceable by other actions in creating benefits or incurring harms. Fourth, either the benefit or harm, though equivalent in principle to each other, is actually stronger due to corroboration by other social indicators. Finally, a benefit or harm may demonstrate definitiveness and certainty, whereas the other is indefinite and uncertain.[285]

Ibn Ashur also highlighted important distinctions in the classification of benefits. Generally, there are three classifications of benefits or interests including those based on impact which is related to necessities, needs and luxuries; scope or universality which is related to the number of individuals compassed; and certainty which is related to the extent of confidence in a benefit, i.e., certain, probable or illusory.[286] He further noted that interests were classified into public and private. The public interest "consists of what is beneficial and useful for the whole or most of the community, and does not concern individuals only insofar as they are members of the whole."[287] Private interest "is concerned with the righteousness and goodness of the individual's acts as a means to the righteousness and wellbeing of the whole society to which they belong."[288]

Also useful to this discussion is al-Qaradawi's work on the jurisprudence of priorities (*al-awlawiyyāt*), change (*taghyīr*) and balance and trade-offs (*fiqh al-muwāzanāt*).[289] The jurisprudence of priorities emphasizes the importance of acting on what is obligatory (*wājib*) and guarding against what is prohibited (*ḥarām*). Moreover, al-Qaradawi emphasized that fiqh provides the general guidelines for the determination of priorities. Thus, the public interest is prioritized over private, long term interests are prioritized over short term, and definite outcomes are prioritized over doubtful outcomes.[290] The jurisprudence of change relates to what must remain stable versus what is amenable to dynamism. Finally, regarding the jurisprudence of balance and tradeoffs, he explains that benefits must be systematically weighted and compared allowing the pursuit of certain benefits over others. Similarly, harms must be weighted and compared in such a way that indicates what can be avoided and what cannot be. Benefits and harms must also be weighted and compared against each other to determine when the avoidance of a harm should be given priority over the pursuit of a benefit or alternatively when a harm must be tolerated to achieve a desired benefit.[291] These contributions are insightful, however, they do not tell us how to establish appropriate boundaries for governance and policy decisions. For that we must examine the concept of ummah.

Ummah

Even before the determination of benefits and harms, it is necessary to determine whose benefits and harms count. The philosophy of *tawḥīd* ensures that all life is viewed as sacred which makes the determination of whose interests count and whose do not especially challenging. Moreover, do governance and public policy in Islam only consider human beings? Which ones? Or is there a basis for broader concerns? Does the Shariʿah only address current generations or are there ethical dimensions related to future ones as well? The determination of who is in and who is out is related to our understanding of the key concept of ummah. Very generally an ummah is a community.

It is often used to refer exclusively to the global Muslim community of the past, present and future. Most jurists and scholars, however, limit their pronouncements to Muslims within a specific geographic area. This may be appropriate for the application of religious law but it is not satisfactory for governance where not only diversity rules but where the main concern is with the public interest. The Shariʿah addresses this concern by pointing to three other significant understandings. The first is related to the community of believers, all believers. The second is concerned with communities that are bound politically and geographically and who share common values and needs, irrespective of belief. And the third, is related to the use of the concept in relation to other living creatures.

The original unity of believers is verified in the Qur'an that describes all believers as a single ummah (*al-Baqarah*: 213). In the Qur'anic chapter titled *al-Anbiyā'* (The Prophets) the stories of Abraham, Lot, Isaac, Noah, David, Solomon, Job, Ismail, Idrīs, Dhū al-Kifl, Jonah, Zachariah, John, Mary and Jesus are recounted to illustrate the unified origins of belief. It states: "Verily, this is your *ummah, one ummah...*" (*al-Anbiyā'*: 92; *al-Mu'minūn*: 52). The believers are in their essence one nation that spans time and space including very diverse people with different temperaments, missions, races, languages, histories, contexts and locations and yet they are described as one ummah, united by belief and service to God.

This understanding is reinforced by the definition of righteousness in the Qur'an, which emphasizes the shared values and ethical actions of believers. It states:

> ... righteousness is to believe in God and the Last Day, and the angels, and the Book, and the messengers. And to spend of your wealth out of a love for Him, for kin and orphans and the needy and travelers and for those who ask and for releasing the indentured. To establish prayer and give *zakat* [mandatory percentage of wealth]; and those who fulfill their commitments when they commit; and those who are patient in sorrow and pain and during fear; these are the people truth; these are the people who are heedful (*al-Baqarah*: 177).

This necessarily includes a wide scope of believers from different faiths. Those identifying as Jews, Christians and whoever else believes in God and the Last Day and undertakes good works fall within this understanding of righteousness (5:69). The Qur'an calls believers to congregate over a word that is common, that is, to worship none other than God (*Āl ʿImrān*: 64) and thereafter to leave the judgment of all other differences to Allah and His Prophet (*al-Nisā'*: 59).

The moderate or just ummah is not exclusive to Muslims. The Qur'an does say that through God's guidance He made Muslims a moderate ummah so that they may be witnesses over people (*al-Baqarah*: 143) but it also states that among the Jews and the Christians are moderate and just ummahs as well.[292] Within each faith are individuals and groups who stand by peace, mercy, moderation and justice. These individuals and groups unite across all faiths to define an ummah that calls for what is beneficial and prohibits what is harmful.

The Qur'an tells us that if God had willed He would have made us all one ummah, but that He might test each with what they were given (*al-Mā'idah*: 48). All of humanity is granted an appointed term on this earth both as individuals and as communities (*Yūnus*: 49). The key is to heed the injunction for *shūrā*, establishing respect and giving each the opportunity to contribute toward the welfare of the whole. Pluralistic engagement is a hallmark of the Shariʿah irrespective of the history of Muslims and their contemporary predicament.

The Qur'an clearly states that for each community is a way that best combines with their dispositions and directions in this world. Differences may on some occasions be a cause for strife especially when approached with pride (*al-Anbiyā'*: 93; *al-Mu'minūn*: 53) but their primary role is to generate new and useful ideas and to seek innovative solutions to common challenges. In other words, the existence of different faiths must not affect the capacity and willingness to unite over beneficial actions. The Qur'an is clear and consistent in its exhortation that differences in belief be left to ultimate arbitration and that the challenge of earthly cooperation in matters of a collective nature ought to be humanity's primary concern (*al-Baqarah*: 113). On a general level, people can unite over mutually beneficial principles of peace, justice, mercy and welfare. More specifically, we can cooperate in a number of policy spheres including commerce, culture, defense, health, environment, innovation, etc.

This discussion begs the question of non-believers. Can they partake in a definition of ummah? While it is clear that the ummah described above is defined by the basic belief in God and a day of judgement, its relations and interactions with non-believers are not qualitatively different from what ought to exist among each other. Here the fundamental premise is not necessarily belief in God but an understanding of humanity and a commitment to comprehensive peace (*al-Nisā'*: 90). All humanity originated from a single soul or being (*al-Anᶜām*: 98; *al-Aᶜrāf*: 189). This is the first and foremost premise that establishes the intimate relationship between all of humanity. It is not a cliché to state that human beings constitute one family, interconnected over time and space. The Qur'an states: "Oh people, We have created you from male and female and have made you into ethnicities and tribes so that you may get to know each other. Truly the most dignified among you in the sight of God is the most heedful. God is knowing and acquainted" (*al-Ḥujurāt*: 13).

Believers are commanded to be righteous and equitable toward all peace-loving people irrespective of belief as God loves those who are equitable (*al-Mumtaḥanah*: 8). Independent of faith, an ummah can be bound by politics, geography, common values and needs. This was the rationale of Prophet Muhammad's community in Madinah. Because of the lack of a common agreement over religion, a social pact was promulgated as outlined in the Constitution or Scroll of Madinah that defined communal relationships between the groups living in the city. The pact served to unite people with diverse beliefs and ethnicities under a banner of peace and common security while encouraging every social group to practice what benefitted itself and the whole community and prohibiting what harmed or did injustice to itself and the wider community. It was an approach that emphasized the characteristics of a robust and inclusive majority bound by the desire to live in peace and prosperity as opposed to an emphasis on minorities that neglected the moral, spiritual and physical extension of individuals and groups beyond narrow identities. Like this historic example, an ummah can certainly be defined politically and geographically. Indeed, in many cases it must be for policy and governance determinations.

The Shariʿah acknowledges the importance and significance of boundaries and borders. Among the concepts used in the Qur'an is that of '*balad*' which can be understood as a defined geographic region with certain specificities and populations.[293] Thus, prophet Ibrahim said: My Lord, make this *balad* secure and endow its people with harvests..." (*al-Baqarah*: 126). In another instance, the Qur'an tells us of the unsurpassed construction acumen of the people of ʿAd, "the like of which was not created in other *bilād* [plural of *balad*]" (*Al-Fajr*: 8). And yet other verses explain both materially and metaphorically how the forces of nature alter and impact the productive capacities and qualities of different *bilād* (*al-Aʿrāf*: 57,58).

Whether referring to the physical concept of borders or the moral boundaries (*ḥudūd*) of God, policy and governance in Islam acknowledge the indispensability of boundaries and their necessity for planning action, establishing the limits of responsibility and the imposition of sanction in governance. Islam's second and most celebrated caliph ʿUmar, who was based in Madinah, had once lamented, "If a baby goat (kid) perishes along the shores of the Euphrates, ʿUmar will be held to account for her on the Day of Resurrection."[294] Responsibility necessitates a determination of boundaries within which effort is exercised and beyond which effort (or lack thereof) is no longer subject to sanction. That said, *tawḥīd* is not intended to make the determination of harms and benefits impossible but rather to act as a guide for the formulation of policies and establishment of governance structures that respect its ethical demands as far as practicable.

Beyond Anthropocentrism

Deeper reflection on ʿUmar's statement above provides a clear indication that Islamic ethics are not anthropocentric. The ethical system elaborated in the Qur'an is comprehensive and as such coverage is provided for all of God's creation. It exhorts people to envision the spiritual dimension of all creation, worthy – if not of dignity – then of protection and awe. The Qur'an is adamant about this and while dignifying the children of Adam nevertheless positions them among a magnificent web of life. Our inability to grasp this reality not only as

Muslims, but also as human beings has led to a myopic and dangerous vision for our collective future. Humanity is dependent on much more than humans. The superficiality of a significant portion of fiqh in this regard – not necessarily due to the superficial minds of jurists and scholars, but rather the pre-programmed approach they take to religious scholarship has rendered ethical concerns marginal to broader, more complex public affairs. It has also undermined the search for alternative approaches and narratives presented in the Qur'an that are available for the enhancement of our collective existence. The *maqāṣid* literature is attempting to remedy this unfortunate predicament, but it remains peripheral to mainstream fiqh, pushing its way into the public sphere, cautious not to offend its mainstream patron. Even as it takes a bolder stand, it is itself reluctant to introspect, to explore the full extent of a comprehensive ethics and confidently assert its conclusions to the world.

The main idea of this discussion is to posit that the promotion of benefits and prevention of harms cannot be limited to humans and even then must be nuanced among them. The human element is only a purposeful link, a means to realize an ultimate objective. This has significant implications for decision-making at various levels, in different spheres and over time. It influences the impact of current decision-making on future outcomes by changing our perception of, and hence responsibility toward, other creation.

Unfortunately, the traditional *maqāṣid* approach which emphasizes the preservation of faith, life, mind, progeny, wealth and dignity reinforces the anthropocentric approach as the value of all creation is measured against human essentials and needs. Benefits and harms are assessed in terms of the values that human beings attach to them. In other words, everything in the universe is perceived, positioned and potentially protected in relation to human needs and not in accordance with any intrinsic value it may have independent of humans. The Qur'an, however, informs people about the value of other creation, i.e., not its value to us but its value in the Divine scheme of which we are only one element. This knowledge makes us accountable for the impact that our choices have on other species and life forms.

Deeper analysis and introspection is required to understand how the Qur'an positions human beings so that they respect, guard and sanctify all creation. The welfare of other life forms and the health of our planet have all but fallen off the Islamic agenda. Islamic discourse is overwhelmed with strictly human affairs and generally a very narrow view of those affairs. The universe in which human existence and livelihood are situated and dependent is hardly given attention except as evidence of the perfection of creation and signs of the surety of the existence of God. The adage that one has only to observe to believe is oft repeated and though this is mentioned in the Qur'an (e.g., *al-Mulk*: 4) it is intended to instigate scientific inquiry and exploration as well as to raise awareness of our responsibilities. The Qur'an teaches that the value of creation is not subject to human calculation, but rather is intrinsically valuable in and of itself. All animals form communities like ours (*ummam amthālukum*) and all creation has a spiritual dimension that we cannot fully appreciate given human limitations. In what follows, we will elaborate on this reality directly from the Qur'an.

There are three particular concepts that have a strong bearing on our understanding of the comprehensiveness of Qur'anic ethics. These include *khilāfah*, *taskhīr* and *takrīm*, all of which require better understandings based on a renewed and integrated reading of the Qur'an. God's statement that He is placing a *khalīfah* on the earth is often taken to mean the vicegerency of humans (*al-Baqarah*: 30). A vicegerent is regarded as an earthly representative of God, which is something that the Qur'an and Sunnah never mention. Likewise, the *takrīm* or dignification of the children of Adam, is not intended to establish human beings as central and supreme beings on earth but rather to exact gratitude for God's favors on humanity. Finally, *taskhīr* understood as the malleability or subservience of the elements of nature does not mean uniquely created to serve humanity and does not exclude the existence of inequality among individuals and groups so that they may benefit from each other. These misunderstanding have not only shaped the Islamic religious experience but have seriously and negatively impacted the way we are in the world and our determination to protect the planet and all of its diversity as an integral dimension of *tawḥīd*.

Khilāfah

The concept of *khilāfah* is perhaps one of the most politically charged concepts in recent history. Although several prominent Islamic scholars both in the past and present understand the concept simply to mean human succession on earth, others have popularized the notion that *khilāfah* entails the vicegerency of man, or God's representative on earth.[295] For the politically and often violently inclined, the concept conjures a specific system of government based on an imaginary caliphate that harkens to a bygone era of male dominance and coercive *religious* rules. There is no basis for this latter understanding of the concept in the Shariʿah. In fact, there are a number of indications that humans are merely successors to whatever may have preceded us on this earth. There is no indication in the Qur'an or Sunnah that any human being, no matter how powerful, was or is God's representative on earth. Even the most elevated of humanity, namely, the prophets and messengers are never referred to as representatives of God.

A stark evidential support for this view is found in the response of the angels when God informs them that He is placing a successor (*khalīfah*) on earth. They retort rather readily by asking: "... will you place therein one who will corrupt her and shed blood?" (*al-Baqarah*: 30). Although the Qur'an tells us that the angels reconsidered their position on the matter after they had witnessed something of Adam's capacities (*al-Baqarah*: 32), their initial reaction does not support the view that the *khalīfah* is anything akin to God's representation on earth. If anything, their concern demonstrates that the introduction of human beings to the earthly system may not be so beneficial. Surely, this would not have been their reaction had they perceived of humans as representatives of God.

The Qur'an tells us that God bequeaths the earth to whomever He wills, so that He may see how people act (*al-Aʿrāf*: 128-129). He says in the Qur'an: "We did offer the Trust to the skies and the earth and the mountains, but they declined to bear it and feared it; but man bore it, he was unjust and ignorant" (*al-Aḥzāb*: 72). Indeed, the assumption of this trust appears to turn the tables on humanity's self-centered perceptions. We are all guests on this earth, here for a short time and then gone, but our duties and custodianship are serious commitments. The earth was created in truth, beauty, absolute perfection and orderliness, a sure proof of the existence of God (*al-Raʿd*: 2-5; *al-Mulk*: 3-4). The earth and its magnificence are spiritual and sensory evidence and reminders for every human being (*Qāf*: 8). The value of human beings as individuals and communities is measured in accordance to their relationship to nature and not vice versa.

The Qur'an drives this point home quite clearly on several occasions. God says that he can end our term whenever He wills and bring about another creation (*Yā Sīn*: 16). Indeed, "Your Lord is self-sufficient and full of mercy. If He pleased, He could remove you and put others in your place, just as He produced you from the offspring of other people" (*al-Anʿām*: 133). Believers are commanded to be righteous and to give generously, but for those who withhold, God warns that He will succeed them with those who will certainly not betray this trust (Muhammad: 38). These verses indicate that humans are certainly not God's representatives on earth but rather that human value is measured against its guardianship of what God has entrusted with it. Short of passing this test and proving sincerity, humans are an expendable element in the Divine scheme.

Takrīm

Dignity is defined as the "quality of being worthy of honor or respect."[296] God says: "We dignified the children of Adam and carried them in the land and the sea; and granted them from all that is good and fair; and preferred them over much of what we created with notable preference" (*al-Isrā'*: 70). Of all of God's creation human beings have an honorable status. This, however, does not translate into an unqualified superiority. Even the content of this verse should demonstrate this assertion. God says He preferred human beings *over much of what He created*, which is certainly not equivalent to *all*. Of the wisdom that God reveals in the Qur'an, we are told: "And do not walk on the earth with insolence, for you cannot penetrate its depths nor can you reach the height of mountains" (*al-Isrā'*: 37).

In addition to the grandeur of the universe, it is notable that animals constitute an important dimension in Qur'anic narratives, metaphors, similitudes and commands. Several chapters of the Qur'an have animal names for titles. Animals, including insects, are presented as creatures that are Divinely inspired (*al-Naḥl*: 68; *al-Naml*: 18-19). The Qur'an tells us that there is not a creature in the earth or in the skies that does not form communities like ours (*al-Anᶜām*: 38). It even exhorts humans to learn from them both by studying their behavior as well as by direct contact and communication (*al-Mā'idah*: 31). Both prophets David and Solomon perfectly understood animals, communicated with them, and employed them in their service (*al-Naml*: 16-22). Prophet Muhammad also understood animals and when his Companions stated that his camel was "stubborn," he responded by telling them that this was not part of her character. Indeed, the camel's sense was a trusted guide in several situations. Modern science continues to unravel these possibilities but we are very far from the understanding presented in the Qur'an.

The Qur'an tells us in a significant number of verses that all creatures in the skies and on earth worship God and glorify His praises (*al-Anbiyā'*: 19; *al-Ḥadīd*: 1; *al-Ḥashr*: 24). In fact, several chapters open with this statement.[297] Moreover, every creature knows its unique prayers and praises and God is cognizant of what they do (*al-Nūr*: 41) and to Him everything, not only humans, will return (*al-Anᶜām*: 38). The fact that we do not understand their mode of worship does not negate its existence (*al-Isrā'*: 44). Indeed, the mountains and the birds echoed God's praises with prophet David (*Ṣād*: 18-19; *Saba'*: 10). We are also told that the trees, sun, stars, moon, thunder and all created matter glorify God (*al-Raḥmān*: 6; *al-Raᶜd*: 13). It is of little surprise that God does not disdain from giving the example of a gnat (*al-Baqarah*: 26), which is not only critical for the sustenance of the universal web of life but is part of a chorus that praises God. Every aspect of creation has intrinsic value in the Divine scheme.

This reality has warranted very strict Qur'anic injunctions when it comes to the protection of non-human creation. Animals are not to be harmed in any avoidable way. In a Prophetic narration, we are told that God curses those who make a target out of anything with a spirit.[298] Animals are not to be branded as God curses those who brand.[299] They are not to be hunted for game. They are further not to be subject to superstitious practices (*al-Mā'idah*: 103; *al-Anᶜām*: 143-

144). Moreover, the principle of proportionality demanded in human responses toward each other (*al-Naḥl*: 126) is also demanded in interactions between humans and animals. Even if an ant stings you and you instinctively kill it, you are not permitted to kill other ants indiscriminately as enjoined in a Prophetic narration in which an ant stung one of the prophets so he ordered the ant colony be burned. In response God revealed to him: Because of an ant's bite you have burnt a community from amongst the communities which sings My glory.[300]

The seriousness of the protection of animals among other creation is also evident in the severity of punishments that both the Qur'an and Prophetic narrations convey. When the people of Thamud killed God's she-camel, after prophet Saleh had instructed them about her watering rights and mandatory protection, the Qur'an tells us that they were utterly destroyed (*al-Shams*: 11-14). In two other well-known Prophetic narrations, we are reminded of the evil fate of the woman who confined a cat without food or water until it died, and the blessed fate of a man who quenched the thirst of a dog by fetching it water from a well.[301]

Human dignity is not an unqualified event. It is an achievement. The Qur'an describes those who do not understand as more misguided than cattle (*al-Furqān*: 44). This is because human beings are at the very least given potentially higher capacities than animals. Yet many refuse to fully exercise their faculties and hence limit their capacities to comprehend certain truths. The worst of creatures, the Qur'an tells us, are those who reject faith given its potential implications for our earthly relationships with each other and with other creatures (*al-Anfāl*: 55-56). Not utilizing our full human potential renders us lower than animals in the Divine scheme (*al-Aʿrāf*: 179). Human dignity is associated with knowledge, stewardship and generosity not control, domination and greed.

Taskhīr

Taskhīr is commonly understood to mean that everything on earth was created to serve humanity in one way or another. Although the Qur'an does state: "Do you not see that God has made subservient to you what is in the skies and what is in the earth, and saturated you with His blessings outwardly and inwardly? ..." (*Luqmān*: 20) this does not imply exclusivity. Everything is created to serve and worship God, but Divine providence purposefully designed the universe in such a way that facilitates and beautifies the human experience (*al-Aʿrāf*: 32). Our ability to enjoy and utilize various elements of creation does not reflect its ultimate value or purpose (*al-Baqarah*: 164).

The earth was in existence before the placement of humans on it. The Qur'an tells us that the skies and earth and everything in between them were created in truth for an appointed term (*al-Aḥqāf*: 3). To God belongs the dominion of heaven and earth and what is between them and what is underneath the soil (*al-Nūr*: 42; Ta-Ha: 6). It is He who has expanded the earth and placed firm mountains and planted everything therein in due measure (*al-Ḥijr*: 19). And it is He that reduces the land from its edges (*al-Raʿd*: 41) in conformance to His *sunnah* that everything belongs to Him and must in time return to Him. The Qur'an states that what He placed on earth is an adornment *for her* so that He may test people as to who is best in conduct (*al-Kahf*: 7). Without this caretaking function, the earth is prone to all sorts of degradation (*al-Kahf*: 8). Based on these assertions, it is safe to say that the earth itself has intrinsic value in the Divine scheme, independent of humanity.

There is nothing to indicate that the earth was created exclusively for human beings or that it required their presence. The earth was arranged in perfection and beauty for all creatures (*al-Raḥmān*: 10). Everything in the skies and the earth depend on God for their needs: "On Him depends all creatures in the heavens and on earth; [and] every day He manifests Himself in yet another [wondrous] way" (*al-Raḥmān*: 29). And God provides sustenance for all His creation (*Hūd*: 6). In light of this, human beings are no less subservient to each other and to other creatures in this Divine scheme than such creation is subservient to them.

The Qur'an states that God has raised some people above others in ranks so that we may be able to commission each other in various ways (*al-Zukhruf*: 32). This does not entitle some to dominate and enslave others. To the contrary, those who have an *upper hand* have higher responsibility and accountability. It is our responsibility to recognize the existence of inequality as a characteristic of diversity. By definition diverse objects cannot be equal. Considering that diversity is a hallmark of creation and a necessity of an interdependent universe where everything plays a unique role in the web of life, inequality must be perceived as a blessing. Humans exhibit an infinite array of diversities. The Qur'an tells us that to each is a specific disposition and tendency to which he or she turns, in order that they may excel in what is beneficial given who they are, whether as individuals, groups or nations. It is not in spite of but because of diversity and inequality that species develop resilience. More often than not, however, inequalities are reinforced not as blessings in a society but to oppress and demean people. This is because dominant individuals and groups lack a comprehensive understanding of human welfare.

While inequality permits *taskhīr* it also poses a great challenge for humanity. The number of verses in the Qur'an that exhort mercy, justice, goodness and welfare by individuals and larger social units both directly and indirectly through narratives and metaphors is too voluminous to cite. Believers are commanded not only to undertake what is good and beneficial but also to enjoin such acts and they are to avoid what is reprehensible while also proscribing it (*Āl ʿImrān*: 104, 110). Whether it is as individual men and women or larger social units, and irrespective of social status related to wealth or education, believers are guardians of one another in this regard (*al-Tawbah*: 71). They are commanded to give to kindred, the needy and travelers (*al-Rūm*: 38) in addition to those who ask and the deprived (*al-Dhāriyāt*: 19). Naturally, those who have been granted more are commanded to give more and as such shoulder a greater responsibility (and burden) than individuals, groups or nations who have relatively less. All provisions must meet acceptable standards that conform to contemporary understandings of human dignity. The Qur'an tells people to give only what they themselves would accept (*al-Baqarah*: 267-268) and reinforces this by stating that righteousness is only attained when people give of what they love (*Āl ʿImrān*: 92).

Whether among each other or among human beings and nature, Qur'anic ethics demand utmost respect and protection. Inequalities in nature, dispositions, skills, capacities, strengths, etc., are not grounds for discrimination, everyone must be treated equitably and given equal opportunity (*ʿAbasa*: 1-12). Instead of disadvantage, inequality must be viewed as a facilitative mercy for the advancement of life. Realizing this mercy demands the construction of robust systems of governance and public policies that protect citizens from the arbitrary exercise of power and the vagaries of wealth while also protecting non-human life forms from human excess. The Qur'an draws attention to an important reality in this regard, i.e., ethical government does not necessarily mean religious government or vice versa. In fact, political power and piety are often separate in Qur'anic narratives as discussed in the final chapter.

Conclusion

Governance and public policy in Islam are guided by a comprehensive ethics that posits *tawḥīd* or unification as its core philosophy. *Tawḥīd* implies that a belief in one God carries with it the responsibility of guarding an order that He ultimately rules. Everything in His order possesses its own sanctity, which is independent of the value attached to it by humans. The blessing of human dignity that is effected through an order that is malleable and responsive to human actions that necessarily impact other creation therefore demands a concern for consequences.

Systematic ethical analysis necessarily involves consideration of the nature and sources of benefits and harms in the Shariʿah. In conformance with the depth and breadth of the Shariʿah and the complexity of *tawḥīd*, policy has to adopt sophisticated and inclusive ethical approaches. But before such calculations are made, questions must be settled regarding whose interests count in any policy discussion. The ummah is a useful concept for this purpose. Although it has traditionally been understood as an exclusively Muslim collective, the Qur'an Sunnah, and early Islamic rule present us with much richer possibilities. Indeed, an ummah can be considered at many levels and is even used to describe communities in the animal kingdom.

This chapter therefore argued that governance and public policy in Islam must move beyond the erroneous anthropocentric view that has been propagated and embedded in the Muslim psyche by traditional scholarship. All creation has intrinsic value in the Divine scheme and we must strive our utmost to protect life in all of its forms. The ethical system in the Qur'an recognizes and sanctifies the interdependency among all creation. While this may prolong and complicate decision-making processes, the practical ethics elaborated in the Qur'an, whose presentation was beyond the scope of this chapter, make the challenge more manageable. In the meantime, what people lack in knowledge ought to be compensated for through faith and trust in a Divine guidance that is wise and all-knowing.

IV

Past Lessons and Future Possibilities

7

Public Policy in Islam as a Process of Reform and Renewal

> Corruption has arisen on land and sea due to what people have earned; so that they may taste some of what they did, perchance to reconsider.
>
> *AL-RŪM*: 41

It is Divine law that God does not exhaust a community that strives to reform and fix its affairs: "For, never would thy Sustainer destroy a community for wrong [beliefs alone] so long as its people behave righteously [towards one another]" (*Hūd*: 117). This highlights the importance that Islam places on the actualization of values such as equity, mercy and justice whether as individuals, groups, communities or nations. The defense of equity in all public affairs is emphasized throughout the Qur'an. Generally, any policy that is guided by *maqāṣid al-sharīʿah* is expected to defend the weak and oppressed even if they do not originate from the same locale or community or share the same faith. Individuals and groups must always be willing to stand up for what is right sometimes irrespective of the worldly consequences (*Hūd*: 116). The Qur'an states: "...And were it not for God's checking one people by means of another, the earth would have been corrupted..." (*al-Baqarah*: 251). This balance is effected by good governance and leadership, wisdom, ethical application of knowledge and when necessary armed defense (*al-Baqarah*: 251).

This chapter argues that from its inception the Shariʿah is about the achievement of social justice, which is understood as the equitable distribution of opportunities, wealth and privileges within a society in accordance with the fundamental principle of human dignity. It starts with a discussion of the relationship between power and piety in the

Qur'an to demonstrate how the distinction between the two suggests that the introduction and application of Qur'anic ethics is a collective responsibility and does not presuppose Islamic political leadership or statehood. The history of the introduction of Islam to Arabia offers a rich and detailed account of the stages and nature of a comprehensive process of social reform. The preponderance of Muslim authority as a result of this process is not to be understood as an end in itself and hence as an unqualified drive for statehood, but rather a consequence of the appeal of Islam to local subjects and its utility in addressing the social challenges of the time. The early recipients of this message understood that the greater part of *Dīn*, the Islamic faith, is a time bound articulation and expression of the Shariʿah for the purpose of achieving equity given prevailing conditions.

An instructive Prophetic narration confirms this understanding: "Verily God sends to this *Ummah* at the head of every one hundred years those who will renew the *Dīn* for it."[302] A century is a period of time where significant changes in our circumstances and knowledge warrant a rereading of the word as evidenced by the circumstances of the world. It is a time limit beyond which our ethical perspectives are outdated, warranting a renewed reading that reflects the state of our knowledge in terms of technological, political, economic and social fields of action, which permit new understandings of how the Revealed and unrevealed word must combine to advance life. Renewal of the *Dīn* cannot be undertaken in the absence of contemporaneous readings of the Revealed and unrevealed word. In the absence of which the *Dīn* becomes archaic, irrelevant and even dangerous by continually rebirthing historic readings that cannot but contribute to civilizational contradictions and backwardness.

This final chapter is divided into three parts. In the first part, I suggest that power and piety are rarely combined in Qur'anic narratives to express the variety of possibilities for good and bad governance in reality and the ways of dealing with both. Civic engagement emerges as a key consequence of such realities. In part two, I examine Islam's action orientation. I argue that action and achieving benefits is critical in the preservation of *Dīn*. The last section then demonstrates how social action is possible even in what appears to be the most intractable circumstances by presenting the timeless lessons of social reform evident from Islam's early history.

Power and Piety in the Qur'an

One of the most striking conclusions that one reaches after a reading of the Qur'an is the clear separation between political power and piety or more generally ethical behavior. This has important implications for governance, public policy in Islam and civic engagement in Islam. Fundamentally, it demonstrates that the actors championing the guidance provided in the Shariʿah can be located within the system of governance itself or within civil society. The locus of actors necessarily defines possible approaches and the nature and extent of responsibility. This separation of power and piety also highlights the importance of establishing institutions that serve to mitigate unethical behavior irrespective of the alleged religious affiliation of a government or its leadership.

Power in the Qur'an is first and foremost defined as the ability to do absolutely everything. This kind of power is only within the purview of God (*al-Mā'idah*: 120). The ultimate source of power is God. He is the Lord of the worlds, Master of the Day of Judgment (*al-Fātiḥah*: 4). In the words of al-Ghazali, "He is the Master of humans, animals, plants, angels, planets, stars, systems, the seen and the unseen. Everything that has existed or shall ever exist in this world is subordinate to God, subservient to Him, bound to His power, and totally dependent upon His grace, blessings, and compassion."[303] He is the source of power, the giver of power and the taker of power. His power is all encompassing.

Human power is necessarily dependent on its Divine source. The narratives in the Qur'an reveal that human power is defined as the ability and willingness to exercise the skills, talents, knowledge, resources and natural endowments that in combination give a person or group advantage over others, thus enabling those with an advantage to dominate and regulate the affairs of others in ways that serve specific interests. This power, although granted by God, is not necessarily related to or representative of Him as already explained in the previous chapter. In fact, associating any individual with Divine representation is particularly serious in public affairs as no one has the right to claim to represent God. The motivation to do so can only be suspect since policies that promote public interests (*al-maṣlaḥah*), respect human dignity (*al-karāmah*) and advance life (*al-iḥyā'*)[304] should not require resort to authoritarianism and supernatural phenomena.

Moreover, even the greatest human power has its limits. Humans cannot alter the laws of nature, foresee the future or control macro social cycles. The Qur'an challenges any power to cause the sun to rise from the west (*al-Baqarah*: 258), create the semblance of a fly (*al-Ḥajj*: 73), calm the seas or the winds, or control the clouds and rainfall. It also explains that days of plenty and hardship are circulated among people (*Āl ʿImrān*: 140) and that the rise and fall of nations is evident for those who observe and travel throughout the earth (*Āl ʿImrān*: 137-139). Every nation eventually succumbs to the causes of decay, and like any other organic phenomena disintegrates and dies.

The Qur'an warns of four major ethical failings or phenomena of political systems and the societies they govern that inevitably lead to self-destruction. These phenomena, which are particularly resistant to authoritative interventions include: (1) economic structures that privilege the powerful few including inequitable income and goods distribution, unfair market regulations, the allowance of certain goods, services or other transactions that are immoral or that promote immorality, and excesses against nature and other living creatures; (2) social structures that privilege certain individuals or groups over others, whether based on gender, race, creed or any other division that subjects one or several groups to the tyranny of another; (3) sexual mores that reflect an intentional neglect of rules of discretion and privacy to exploit a specific element in society, appease particular constituencies, or support unlawful gains; and (4) religious convictions and innovations that attribute any of the above or any other false claims to the Divine. The gradual permeation throughout society of human lapses associated with these choices leads to a betrayal of human dignity and an accumulation of injustices in diverse manifestations. That said, God grants power to whom He wills, be they rich or poor, pious or rebellious, believing or disbelieving, benevolent or repressive, etc., for as long or as little as He wills. The Qur'an states:

"God, You are the proprietor of the Dominion, You grant dominion to who You will, and You seize if from who You will, and You honor who You will, and You disgrace who You will, in Your hand is all good, and You are over everything capable" (*Āl ʿImrān*: 26). In this regard it relates several illustrative narratives of the possible combination of power and piety. Prophet Abraham, for instance, is shown to be dialoguing with a ruler over the existence of God (*al-Baqarah*: 258). The ruler, not identified by name or title to allow generalizations to others in similar positions, demonstrates that belief in God is not a condition for the grant of power. It further illustrates how pride of power is met with Qur'anic ethics through calm and intelligent dialogue.

In another example a prophet of the Israelites appoints Talut as a king over the Israelites despite their displeasure due to his lack of wealth. Talut, however, had been chosen and granted advantage in wisdom, knowledge and physique (*al-Baqarah*: 247). His lack of wealth was not a disadvantage in God's Divine scheme. This does not mean that power is not aided by wealth or that wealth is an unimportant factor, but rather it highlights the fact that wealth is not a precondition for power or effective leadership when other advantages are present.

This is in stark contrast to the spectacular example of Pharaoh and Moses. Pharaoh, identified by his authoritative title as well, was granted extreme power with all of its political, economic and social accoutrements. Yet he transgressed all humanitarian limits by dividing his people in order to subjugate certain groups. Pharaoh enslaved the children of Israel, killing their sons and debauching their women and girls. Prophet Moses and his brother Aaron were tasked with bringing Pharaoh the message of faith so that he may reform and remove the burdens of the Israelites. Throughout this narrative, Pharaoh is addressed by prophet Moses in the most eloquent ways (*Ṭā-Hā*: 50-73).

It is important to recognize that non-believers are not exclusively represented as oppressive tyrants or even as bad leaders. The story of prophet Joseph involves a king who was powerful and benevolent but not a believer. The narrative reveals how the king was ultimately concerned with the welfare of his people through his drive to ensure their long run food security. When he recognizes that prophet Joseph would be the most capable official in this regard, he entrusts him with one of the highest posts of the land. "Be assured this day, you are of high standing with us, invested with all trust" (*Yūsuf*: 54). Thus, the prophet was granted authority over all the storehouses of Egypt so that he could successfully navigate the impending famine (*Yūsuf*: 54-57). Political leadership in this narrative thus combines power with unbelief and benevolence. As a result, prophet Joseph could ably commit to this government and serve a public that was notably unbelieving as well.

In the story of King Solomon there is the combination of extreme power and extreme faith as well as extreme power with unbelief, albeit initially, through the leadership of the Queen of Sheba. Indeed, the King's power extended beyond the human realm to include authority over all creatures (*Saba'*: 12-13; *al-Naml*: 18-22). This narrative illustrates how prophet Solomon, clearly one of the most powerful kings that ever lived, had a diplomatic exchange with another very powerful and benevolent but initially disbelieving Queen. Here too the Qur'an does not identify the Queen of Sheba by name, giving female leadership at the highest level a generic quality. The Qur'an is clear that power is not granted to men only, neither in its worldly sense or its spiritual sense.[305] In fact, the Qur'an clearly demonstrates that the Queen of Sheba ruled over a vast kingdom with prosperity, dignity, and an interesting form of consultative government.[306] When her army commanders assured her that they were "endued with strength and given to vehement war," she wisely responded, "Kings, when they enter a country, despoil it, and make the noblest of its people its meanest, and that is what they do." She therefore opted to make peace with King Solomon (*al-Naml*: 23-44). Al-Ghazali affirms that "history is witness here as elsewhere that women can reach great heights in society with their nobility, magnanimity, and strong belief."[307] These examples are sufficient to demonstrate that power and piety are not always paired, in fact they rarely are.

Even the simplest understanding of the Qur'an cannot deny that God grants power to whomever He pleases be they male or female, rich or poor, good or bad, believing or rebellious and local or foreign. It is also clear that power, politics and piety are not necessarily related in the ways that ethical people may wish them to be. Although constitutive of Divine law, power in the hands of tyrants has led to significant human suffering throughout history. A resort to God and the guidance that He revealed in the Shariʿah is intended to encourage and empower people to stand up for what is right and to redress injustice wherever it is practiced and however they are positioned within their societies. Our understanding of the preservation of *Dīn* is critical for the effective fulfillment of this duty.

Islam's Action Orientation

The preservation of *Dīn* (as the religion of Islam) is the most salient of the six essential *maqāṣid*. All other objectives of the Shariʿah, as classically defined, at any historical moment are necessarily compassed by this supreme objective. In other words, the articulation of the preservation of life, progeny, intellect, dignity and wealth are all expounded and regulated by the prevailing conception of *Dīn*. This means that social reform and redressing injustice are directly related to our understanding and practice of *Dīn*. In light of this, the religion of Islam can be understood to have two major aspects. These are related to what Draz terms the extensive and the intensive or the internal and the external,[308] which appear to coincide with the distinction suggested in the *maqāṣid* literature between the *ʿibādāt* or acts of rituals and devotion and *muʿāmalāt* or worldly dealings. While the intensive only constitutes a relatively limited dimension of Islam albeit in terms of visible manifestation, many scholars have incorrectly insisted that this aspect suffices for *Dīn*.[309] In fact, it is only in the extensive, in worldly dealings, that the sincerity of the intensive can be revealed. In accordance with the Qur'an, anyone who has worked an atom's weight of good will see the implications and consequences of their actions on the Day of Judgement, and anyone who worked an atom's weight of evil will likewise see (*al-Zalzalah*: 7-8). Prophet Muhammad warned that on the Day of Judgment people will have to explain in what occupation they spent their lives, for what motives they acted, from what source they made their fortunes, how they employed their resources and how they used their own bodies.[310]

The preservation of religion thus involves two feats. The first is to guard the principle acts of worship and what they are dependent upon against corruption and innovations. Testifying that there is no deity except God, praying, fasting, giving zakat and the pilgrimage will more or less remain unchanged for all time. The second is to actualize the duties articulated in the Qur'an by internalizing and synthesizing relevant rules with prevailing conditions so that our actions are defined by the basic values of Islam including mercy, equity, justice, wisdom and welfare. Draz has tersely summarized the duties of a believer as follows:

> The care taken to enquire into one's duties and teach others theirs; moral effort; conforming to good examples; balanced actions, which keep to the middle path; righteousness; striving to perform what is good or even best; the most beautiful actions; the best words; sincerity; chastity and decency; the wise personal use of goods honestly acquired; courage, endurance and constancy; gentleness and modesty; circumspection in judgments; doing good in general; doing good to our parents in particular, treating them with honor, obedience, tenderness and concern; treating our spouses well; kind conversation with them and mutual consultation; supporting the needs of our families, in proportion to our resources; paying compensation to divorced spouses; helping your close relatives, near and distant neighbors, travelers, the needy – help which is duly taken from good things that are honestly acquired. Supporting the poor and orphans in times of famine; freeing slaves; uprightness; generosity. Equity, as represented by the vertical balance of the scales, which tilt neither to the right nor to left.
>
> Giving precise statement in all required testimonies, whether it is against our relatives or ourselves; returning what has been entrusted to us to its rightful owner; being faithful to any engagement undertaken, word given, or oath sworn; practicing hospitality and selflessness; tolerating the ill-educated with kindness; returning good for evil; encouraging towards the good and turning away from evil – all believers are united on this point. Encourage harmony and charity; the co-operation of all to help virtue and discipline prevail; mutual

exhortation to patience and mercy; attachment to holy union; consolidating all our sacred links; loving the spiritual community and praying for it (showing community spirit); the wisest and most honest ways of preaching the truth; in brief, all ways of acting which are acknowledged and approved (by reason and tradition).[311]

These are the positive commandments that prescribe or praise certain duties and which are mostly related to individuals but obviously extendable to larger social units. At the state level the Qur'an includes injunctions related to peace making (*al-Ḥujurāt*: 9); mutual defense (*al-Ḥujurāt*: 9); clemency (*al-Mā'idah*: 34); immunity (*al-Tawbah*: 1, 4); asylum (*al-Tawbah*: 6); allowance for probation (*al-Tawbah*: 2); opportunity to avoid hostilities (*al-Tawbah*: 3); safe passage for those not involved in hostilities (*al-Tawbah*: 6); as well as acknowledging people's right to belonging and a homeland (*al-Mumtaḥanah*: 9). The Qur'an also includes negative duties or acts that are forbidden, which Draz summarizes as follows:

to commit suicide; to commit indecent assault or any action leading to crime; to engage in prostitution or fornication, or any other sort of immorality, public or hidden; to lie, to boast, to follow uncontrolled desires, to imitate the unbelievers; to covet other people's goods; to hoard money and love riches excessively; to strut arrogantly; to dress indecently; to make use of ill-acquired gain or employ anything impure (both physically and metaphorically); to commit infanticide (even under the pressure of cruel poverty, whether experienced or anticipated); to show any disrespect to our parents in their older age; to mistreat our spouses (through humiliation, extortion, deprivation or anything else); to shed human blood *which God has expressly consecrated, if it is not by right*; to cause ruin or corruption on the earth; to display aggression, even towards enemies; to use (or worse, appropriate) another person's goods, without their consent; to touch the property of orphans, except in the most honest manner (in order to increase its value for them); to reject orphans; to do any violence to them; to treat them disdainfully; to neglect the poor; to scold people for asking for help; to choose poor-quality objects as gifts; to give false

> witness; to commit any breach of trust; to enter anyone's home without asking their permission and first greeting them; to withdraw from any gathering without permission from the host; to slander other people; derogatory nicknames; to plot an injustice or an act of aggression; to break our sacred links and form schisms...[312]

Again, at the state level the Qur'an includes prohibitions against breaking treaties (*al-Tawbah*: 4); evicting people from their homes (*al-Ḥajj*: 40); and being the first to transgress. All of these duties are integral dimensions of the preservation of *Dīn* and may form the foundation of an ethical and humane public policy. The Qur'an states: "Did you see he who denies the *Dīn*? It is he who repulses the orphan; and does not urge the feeding of the destitute..." (*al-Māʿūn*: 1-4). The most forceful condemnations of failures to act are related to persecution (*al-Baqarah*: 190-91, hunger (*al-Māʿūn*: 3; *Quraysh*: 4), internal displacement (*al-Baqarah*: 85) and forced migration while the most commendable responses include saving lives (*al-Mā'idah*: 32), feeding the hungry and guaranteeing human security (*Quraysh*: 4). The Qur'an, however, is cognizant of the challenging nature of such efforts both in terms of material costs and in the human will to consistently extend relief (*al-Balad*: 4-17).

It is clear that the preservation of religion is inextricably linked to the way we act upon the world. The test of faith is found in action (*al-ʿAnkabūt*: 2-3). To uphold God's religion, is to establish, protect and defend the principles of Islam appropriately and within diverse contexts. Success in the life of this world is contingent upon consistent application of Islam's moral imperatives in times of hardship as well as in times of ease. This Divine expectation forces the believer into a constant struggle to achieve balance between the forces that impact daily life. A continual oscillation between the Revealed word and the world as we experience it daily characterizes the state of a practicing Muslim.

The guidance required to support this struggle (jihad) is found in the command of *tajdīd* or renewal of *Dīn* alluded to by Prophet Muhammad in the statement mentioned above. For every major historical epoch there is a renewed need to translate the intensive and extensive dimensions of Islam into relevant and tangible social action. In our contemporary world, this requires a new fiqh, namely, fiqh *wāqiʿī* or practical fiqh. Knowledge of the Revealed word and its historical significance can at most be considered a theoretical understanding or fiqh *naẓarī*, which constitutes much of what is conveyed by jurists and scholars today.

Likewise to be knowledgeable of the sensory and experiential world can at best be considered an understanding of reality or *fiqh al-wāqiʿ*. Reform and renewal, however, requires an integration of both which gives rise to a practical or realistic understanding or *fiqh wāqiʿī* allowing suitable applications in different contexts.

The early history of Islam is a poignant example of how the nascent Muslim community accomplished this feat and, as a result, was able to change a political system that had disenfranchised and oppressed certain individuals and groups in addition to several of the other injustices noted in the previous section based on tribal customs. The following sections highlight some of the timeless lessons concerning social reform and renewal that are still of relevance today.

Lessons from the Early History of Islam

The message must be truthful, clear, logical and useful: This is one of the greatest lessons of relevance to modern social reform efforts. Although the Qur'an itself was gradually revealed over the course of twenty-three years, it was evident from the very start that its message encompassed these critical characteristics. Starting from the radical premise of human equality, the Qur'an sought to open all avenues of human action to every member of society. In terms of gender parity, for instance, the Qur'an states the following:

> For Muslim men and Muslim women, and believing men and believing women, and devout men and devout women, and persevering men and persevering women, and humble men and humble women, and charitable men and charitable women, and men who fast and women who fast, and men who guard their chastity and women who guard [their chastity], and men who remember God often and women who remember [God often], God has prepared for them forgiveness and a great recompense (33: 35).

This attitude toward gender parity is reaffirmed consistently throughout the Qur'an where female agency and leadership, both spiritual and political, is articulated without qualification. It states: "Believing men and believing women are guardians of one another; they command what is just, and forbid what is evil ..." (*al-Tawbah*: 71). The importance of this element of Islam's message appears just as strong today as it was when it was first revealed.

So important is the premise of human equality that it formed the main focus of Prophet Muhammad's farewell address. On the most sacred day, of the most sacred month, in the most sacred city of Makkah, he reiterated his mission's most important commands stressing that everything he conveyed in this last sermon was as sacred as the time and place in which they were being delivered. He emphasized the sanctity of life, property, fair commerce and public morality. He stressed the importance of partnership and mutual respect between men and women. He also reminded people of their common origin:

> All mankind is from Adam and Eve, an Arab has no superiority over a non-Arab nor a non-Arab has any superiority over an Arab; also a white has no superiority over black nor a black has any superiority over white except by heedfulness toward God (*taqwa*) and good deeds...[313]

The Prophet had clarified that from henceforth only faith combined with good deeds would set people apart. The struggle for human equality during his mission had brought oppression to a minimum, slavery was well on its way to being abolished, overt aggression had been contained and the rights of the weak and marginalized had largely been secured. These foundational tenets, however, are only part of the complex and timeless guidance that constituted completion of *the Dīn* (*al-Mā'idah*: 3).

Our context today allows for ever more sophisticated ways of understanding the principles of the Revealed and unrevealed word. There is not a policy area under consideration today that would not find some form of guidance in the Qur'an. To give one substantial example, let us consider food and agriculture. In simple terms the

Qur'an repeatedly exhorts believers to eat what is "lawful" and "wholesome" (*al-Baqarah*: 168, 172]; *al-Naḥl*: 14). The association of food with spirituality is evident wherever mention of the former is made. Food and more broadly agriculture is also associated with increases in population and the rise of civilizations (*al-Rūm*: 9). The role of agriculture and the quality of human nutrition is fundamental to the construction of stable, healthy and strong communities. Thus, the Qur'anic injunctions and narratives concerning food and agriculture have profound implications for the preservation of life.

Unlike popular understandings that limit rules to food stuff prohibitions and even then mostly to meat and meat byproducts and alcohol, the Qur'an contains a wealth of information of what constitutes wholesome or *ṭayyib* foods as well as the role of food and agriculture in human security. Indeed, issues of nutrition, food security and distribution are clearly delineated in the Qur'an as responsibilities of civil society and the state (*Yūsuf*: 55). This is reinforced through the study of the early days of Islam when Madinah experienced a severe drought during the caliphate of ʿUmar. A comprehensive governance framework was immediately devised that harmonized policies across government to ensure accommodation of the food crisis. Rationing was complemented with requests for aid from neighboring regions, distribution did not favor any individuals or groups over others, and the rules of justice during times of normalcy were suspended to take account of extraordinary human suffering. The Shariʿah makes critical contributions in the areas of food security as well as nutrition and agriculture more generally.

To accept the Qur'anic injunctions to provide and to eat what is lawful and wholesome would change the face of the modern food industry including agriculture, manufacturing, processing, marketing, distribution, and so forth. Rather than accept the status quo, a reading of the word in relation to the world today should encourage us to think of sustainable development alternatives that would not only improve human health but also put less stress on our earth and other creatures that suffer the consequences of immoral human consumption habits. Several areas need immediate attention including distribution and the rights of the less fortunate (*al-Qalam*: 24); waste (*al-Anʿām*:

141); and extravagance (*al-Isrā'*: 27). As for livestock, the concept of *ḥalāl* must be understood with much greater adequacy. A properly run *ḥalāl* enterprise would protect the rights of animals, respect their communal nature, ration their slaughter for only what is necessary, allow them proper living environments and natural feed, guard against waste and generally show mercy. Today's global mass-market livestock industries, including many so-called *ḥalāl* participants, betray the essence of Islam by violating the sanctity of animal life.

Fealty to Islam is based on the acceptance of principles and not loyalty to specific personalities. Beyond the Divinely chosen messengers, leadership is recognized only to the extent that it upholds principles of mercy, equity, wisdom and welfare by synthesizing the rules of the Shariʿah with prevailing contexts so that these principles become the lived experience of all those bound within a specific authoritative structure. When both Abū Bakr and ʿUmar assumed leadership of the Muslim community they demanded allegiance only to the extent that they upheld Islamic principles. In his inauguration address, Abū Bakr stated, "If I do well, help me; and if I do wrong, set me right. Sincere regard for truth is loyalty and disregard for truth is treachery." [314] ʿUmar would later reiterate this sentiment at his inauguration when he affirmed, "I will seek guidance from the Holy Book, and will follow the examples set by the Prophet and Abū Bakr. In this task I seek your assistance. If I follow the right path, follow me. If I deviate from the right path, correct me so that we are not led astray."[315]

Leadership must be meritorious, strong, and committed but not authoritarian: Although principle-based, reform and renewal demands leadership. The model for perfect leadership in this regard is that of Prophet Muhammad. The Qur'an states that he was literally set on the righteous path of all affairs (*al-Jāthiyah*: 18). But despite this, he was not permitted to be authoritarian (*al-Ghāshiyah*: 22) or even to be harsh-mannered (*Āl ʿImrān*: 159). Prophet Muhammad's moral character thus displayed unwavering trustworthiness, honesty, intelligence, patience, insightfulness and decisiveness. He further placed a high premium on consultation and teamwork. Throughout the years before Revelation, he had abstained from many of the social practices that may have been construed as weaknesses in his character or judgment. To this day, the combination of his character with the appeal of Islam's message serves to attract followers while making it exceedingly difficult for his detractors to discredit him.

Prophet Muhammad's form of leadership accommodated the rise of other leaders and outstanding individuals and groups, similar to the messengers who came before him. The Qur'an and Sunnah are replete with such examples. No individual, man or woman, can bring anything meaningful to humanity without the support and cooperation of others. Even the most powerful are dependent upon others. Indeed, the Islamic civilization was built on the cooperation of a man and a woman. Together prophet Abraham and his wife Hajar established the pilgrimage rites of Islam. During Hajj, Muslims trace the footsteps of these two great individuals to earn God's forgiveness. Hajar's repetitive trek between the hilltops of Safa and Marwa convey the essence of Divine law as it applies to the relationship between human effort and prosperity. In its entirety, the story illustrates the trust vested in the agency and faithfulness of women and their indispensable role in the rise of civilizations.

During Prophet Muhammad's mission, Islam witnessed the rise of many great women. Khadījah bint Khuwaylid (d.620) was a successful businesswoman even before marrying Prophet Muhammad. Her marriage to the Prophet would be much celebrated given her social status, success and highly regarded character. Khadījah would earn the honor of becoming the first Muslim. The Prophet would later lament her death by stating that God had not granted him anyone better than her.[316] Another outstanding woman, whom the Prophet married after the death of Khadījah, was ʿĀ'ishah bint Abū Bakr (d. 678). ʿĀ'ishah had a great influence on Islamic scholarship, political life and public affairs especially in the years following the Prophet's death. Indeed, the Qur'an employs an incident that involves ʿĀ'ishah to teach important lessons about social life that include the right of women to secure and free movement (*al-Nūr*: 11-23).

According to the Qur'anic narrative, ʿĀ'ishah was accidently left behind during an expedition after she had gone to search for a necklace. She passed the night at the camp assuming that someone would come back for her. The next morning a Makkan emigrant sighted her and escorted her to the main camp. This gave certain elements in the community cause to gossip and slander ʿĀ'ishah and the Makkan, neither of whom are mentioned by name in the Qur'an so that the lessons of this incident may be generalized in time and space. The seriousness of the accusation as well as its potential consequences for the safety of women and their freedom of movement was clearly and strictly addressed in the Qur'an. By placing blame on those who slandered these two individuals, the Qur'an affirms the protection of a social order that permits women to move about freely without fear of reproach and defamation. There is no concern expressed over any aspect of the behavior of either protagonist in this incident. It is only the community's response that is clearly in violation of the Shariʿah.

This freedom paved the way for women to assume leadership roles and make diverse contributions for the betterment of society. Women independently gave their oath of fealty to Islam to the Prophet, and many emigrated alone from Makkah to Madinah after their conversions to support the new community. Rufaydah bint Saʿad, a skilled nurse, established the first makeshift emergency clinic that tended to the wounded during battle. Nusaybah bint Kaʿab al-Anṣāriyyah (d. 634) and Khawlah bint al-Azwar (d.639) were renowned for their outstanding fighting skills and both participated in major battles alongside the men. This cooperation between men and women continued into the rules of the rightly guided caliphs. ʿUmar, the second caliph, appointed al-Shifā' bint ʿAbdullāh as the first market inspector in Madinah. The position of al-Shifā' involved patrolling the markets looking for any suspicious activity as well as providing advice to merchants who were unsure of the permissibility of certain transactions.[317]

***Not to discount the general public, the elite, or the disabled*:** Social reform initiatives require support from all walks of life. In all ages the followers of the messengers have tended to be the general public who stand to gain the most from changes in the social order. Prophet Muhammad was no exception. The message that he brought aimed to reestablish the Divinely ordained dignity of every human being. This resonated with women, the enslaved, impoverished, weak and marginalized in society. Abū Bakr, who later became the first caliph, would spend great sums of his wealth on freeing men and women from bondage.

Indeed, the history of Islam suggests that a major turning point for the nascent Muslim community occurred when a small group of men from Madinah converted during the pilgrimage season. The group believed that Islam had the potential to end the bitter divisions that were ravaging the clans in Madinah. Their dedication in transmitting the message would see over seventy converts, including women, converge on Makkah to pledge allegiance to the Prophet. The conversion and support of the Madianites would eventually open a safe haven for the Muslims of Makkah and provide a suitable environment for the transformation of the community.

According to al-Ghazali, in Madinah "...were created the first Muslim families, market places, government cadres, centers of learning, trade enterprises, farms, and legislative councils; all under the guidance of Divine Revelation and the enlightened leadership of the exponent of the Revelation, Muhammad."[318]

Beyond ordinary citizens, however, the impact of widespread and deep reform on social and economic structures, as well as on the geopolitical balance of power, demands the support of certain actors in a society's elite. Business and community leaders representing diverse social constituents, members of the creative industries, military personnel, governors, and so forth, provide reform with critical elements of creativity, resources and protection. From the very beginning of his mission, Prophet Muhammad had the solid support of his elderly and venerated uncle, Abū Ṭālib, who notably did not embrace Islam. In fact, several outstanding figures that did not embrace Islam (some only initially) aided the Islamic call, which points to an important lesson. Cooperation can be based on diverse motives so long as the contributions of different actors are clear and the objectives of reform are respected. The Prophet's recourse to Negus, the Christian King of Ethiopia, to provide refuge for the Muslims who could no longer tolerate the intensity of persecution is a case in point.

In fact, the persistence of extreme persecution actually served to attract the sympathy of Islam's most vociferous opponents, Quraysh's elite. Thus, a major setback to the opposition took place when Ḥamzah ibn ʿAbd al-Muṭṭalib, another of the Prophet's uncles, converted in an act of retribution when the Prophet was attacked by one of his other uncles. Ḥamzah's conversion was a strong blow to Quraysh as he was highly regarded for his honesty and strength. Soon after, Quraysh suffered an even heavier loss with the conversion of ʿUmar ibn al-Khaṭṭāb. ʿUmar, who became Islam's second caliph, was a magnanimous character known for his decisiveness and courage. Then there were the conversions of Khālid ibn al-Walīd and ʿAmrū ibn al-ʿĀṣ. The conversion of both these men who had earlier fought against Islam was undoubtedly a very heavy blow to the Quraysh elite demonstrating how a truthful message combined with outstanding leadership and great patience can attract the most unlikely allies. ʿAmrū ibn al-ʿĀṣ was a renowned military commander. He is best known for his conquest of Egypt. Khālid too was a military commander and fighter of mythical magnitude. Commanding armies under Prophet Muhammad and his successors Abū Bakr and ʿUmar, he was one of Islam's most brilliant military tacticians winning every battle that he led. In 636 CE Khālid led the Muslims to victory in the Battle of Yarmouk against the Byzantine Empire, which ended Roman rule over the area known as the Fertile Crescent. He also defeated the Persian army effectively uniting all of Arabia. As a matter of fact, his *stardom* would eventually lead ʿUmar to discharge him due to a concern that the Muslims may attribute victory to Khālid's leadership as opposed to the will of God and thereby be tested in their faith. A lesson that should not be lost on Muslims today as many have come to idolize popular Muslim figures confusing the line between Islam and its leadership.

Evident strength, wealth and talent, however, are not to distract the leaders and champions of reform from engaging all interested stakeholders. The Qur'an makes special mention of the disabled in this regard. In the introduction to *Surah ʿAbasa* (He Frowned) the Qur'an conveys an incident where a poor blind man approached the Prophet for instruction while the latter was engaged with a leader of Quraysh. The Prophet's immediate response was to continue his initial discussion ignoring the blind man, whereupon he received Revelation reproving his reaction. The Revelation warns believers not to discount people on account of their apparent or immediate circumstances. Indeed, it states that we have no way of knowing who will be the true leader or champion of a cause. As it happened, the blind man went on to become a governor of Madinah. In short, every member of society counts.

Economics matter: Most reform measures have economic implications though some greater than others. The impact of reform on economic privileges plays a key role in its rejection or acceptance. Deep reform often involves changing attitudes, material arrangements and eventually rules. The early rejection of Islam by the pagans of Arabia was partly due to the impending loss of economic privilege. In addition to tribal allegiances that allowed a relatively small group of individuals to dominate wealth, the presence of different idols in Makkah further guaranteed a substantial influx of pilgrims with its associated economic and trade benefits. The message of equality and unification brought by Islam promised to change this.

On a purely psychological level, the message emboldened the attitudes of those with humble means as well as those who had been enslaved. No individual was better than any other except by piety and good works. No individual could own or inherit another individual. Every person and every creature had divinely ordained rights that could not be legitimately violated by any other individual or group no matter who they claimed to be. The dignified attitudes to which these basic tenets gave rise, greatly challenged the foundations upon which Arabia's ruling tribes had built their economic system.

It was not long before the new community had the strength to actively target the prevailing economic system through boycotts and sanctions. In particular, the Muslims embarked on a campaign to intercept Quraysh's trade caravans. In doing so, the Muslims hoped to display their strength signaling that impunity would no longer be tolerated. Moreover, it would show Quraysh the vulnerability of its position while compensating for the value of the property that the Makkan converts had lost when they were forcefully driven out of their homes. In fact, the Battle of Badr was instigated by the interception of a major caravan of gold. It was an outstanding victory for the Muslims that served to cement the strength and morale of the nascent community. It was an equally heavy loss for the Makkans in terms of their leadership position in the region, their unrivaled supremacy in matter of faith and most of all their economic dominance. The victory had convinced many that Prophet Muhammad and his followers were set to rule Arabia and perhaps beyond. Tribes from across the region pledged fealty to the Prophet and many entered the fold of Islam.

In addition to changing attitudes and the material arrangements of a society, cementing reform also entails changing the rules. The Qur'an's contribution in this regard is profound. Its economic rules and ethics which constitute a comprehensive system, can have immense impacts on the way people perceive and manage wealth and resources, and consequently on how they interact with their environments. The prohibition against usury[319] (*Āl ʿImrān*: 130; *al-Nisā'*: 161; *al-Rūm*: 39; *al-Baqarah*: 275) while encouraging legitimate trade (*al-Baqarah*: 275) is only one such injunction that has the potential to change the world. So immersed is the global financial system in usurious transactions that we have reached a historical and intellectual impasse. Few can contemplate other possibilities. But rather than uphold God's word, many Islamic scholars have made pronouncements that permit usurious transactions based on a very limited understanding of contemporary economics and finance and the consequences that people around the world have had to suffer on account of laxity regarding this prohibition. The matter in the Qur'an is clear: usury is forbidden from the perspective of the Shariʿah irrespective of the level of interest charged.[320]

Prioritizing peace and respecting pluralism: The Qur'an, Sunnah and governance practices of the early Companions placed special emphasis on the creation and respect of covenants and social pacts of all sorts. Reform cannot be robust when it excludes any of the constitutive elements of a diverse society. Broad social agreements encompass security, social inclusion and goods and services provision for all members of society. In its essence, Islam is in fact a covenant between believers and God. It is fundamentally an agreement that believers will not betray their oath to God after having ratified it, or sever the bonds that God has commanded to be joined, or corrupt the earth (*al-Baqarah*: 27).

All covenants between believers and other people are governed by the primary covenant between them and God (*al-Naḥl*: 91). Covenants are to be made and respected with all people inclined to live in peace (*al-Tawbah*: 4, 7). The fulfillment of agreements is a sacred trust that cannot be rescinded without just cause (*al-Naḥl*: 95). In addition, retaliation for broken agreements by other parties is not permissible unless accompanied with open hostility [by the enemy] (*al-Tawbah*: 12). The early history of Islam is replete with negotiations of peace settlements and non-aggression pacts in conformance with God's command to give peace priority: "And if they [the enemy] incline toward peace, so you too incline toward it, and place your trust in God, it is He Who is the Hearer, the Knower" (*al-Anfāl*: 61).

The example of Madinah is once more instructive. With the arrival of the Makkan converts, Madinah became inhabited by four distinct groups of people including the emigrants of Makkah, the Ansar or helpers of Madinah (Muslim hosts), the pagans and the Jews. The Ansar of Madinah were its original inhabitants, fully settled and attuned to a specific culture. They had addressed their major differences but nevertheless experienced occasional disagreements. The emigrants had come to Madinah needing shelter and sources of income for food and other necessities. They were also experiencing a form of culture shock, as life in Madinah was more relaxed and open than that of Makkah. The pagans could be classified into two groups: those who simply disbelieved and did not care for the beliefs of others, and those who feigned friendship but who held much resentment toward the new arrivals and Islam more generally. Finally, there were the Jews of Madinah who had settled there even before the helpers. They had alliances with the Arab tribes that had settled in Madinah, who had benefited from "their [the Jewish] ways because of the virtue they saw in them that they had acquired through the prophets."[321] The Jews had maintained their unique and largely separate existence. They excelled in finance and economics and dominated trade in a number of strategic commodities. Although Islam brought changes that would impact the customs of all of these groups, though admittedly some more than others, it also mandated respect of legitimate differences. The Prophet was therefore tasked with finding a way to enfranchise all members of this new community.

The result was the Constitution or Scroll of Madinah, which outlined communal relationships between all the groups living in Madinah. The objective of the document was to define an ummah that had a common purpose and defense strategy irrespective of the differences among its members. A kind of social pact, the document was designed to put to ease the minds of those who had not accepted Islam and those of the Jewish communities. It was also to clarify what was acceptable in order to maintain the internal and external security of Madinah. According to the pact, each distinct community within Madinah would be permitted to maintain its current practices and honor blood-money contracts between themselves. Each was mandated to treat its weaker members with mercy and justice. Believers would not be permitted to leave anyone among them burdened by debt, i.e., extending support was obligatory. No member of society was permitted to aid any other member in harming another or in committing any other injustice. The Jews of Madinah were assured that if they acceded to the substance of the agreement they would be aided and treated with justice and equality. Their belief was seen as no different in terms of its ultimate goal of serving God. They were considered one nation or ummah with the believers, though each was to practice its own religion.

In addition to collective defense, all members of the community were expected to counsel each other, do good works and avoid reprehensible behavior. Disputes from henceforth would be referred to God and the Prophet (*al-Nisā'*: 59) who was enjoined by the Qur'an to permit the Jews and the Christians judicial freedom (*al-Mā'idah*: 42-48). With that, Madinah would emerge as a sanctuary for all its residents while defining the ummah through a common goal and the principles of mercy, justice and equality. Like other titles in the Qur'an, Madinah is a generic title meaning town or city, emphasizing the possibility of its replication in time and space.

Armed defense as a last resort: In extreme cases of social reform a call to arms is unavoidable. As the Muslims were shaping their new community, the violence of Quraysh was unrelenting. Nevertheless, the permission to fight the Quraysh only came after the achievement of several important milestones including the establishment of a legitimate political entity; existence of a core message and its deep penetration of hearts and minds; prolonged patience in home territory with heavy sacrifice including a cruel three-year long siege; accession to the cause by outstanding individuals with strong leadership and other skills; multiple emigrations; fortification of the community in Madinah, both in terms of its character but also materially and physically; the formation of alliances with surrounding tribes; and the capacity to fight and withstand war but more importantly the faith to desist and make peace. It was then, and only then, that believers were ready to fight and the community could withstand the impending stress of armed defense.

Thus, while the Qur'an prefers peace, given certain circumstances it does include the command to fight as preferable as peace may be. In the view of al-Ghazali, "peace is to be welcomed when rights are protected and beliefs are respected; but if peace means abject surrender and subjugation, it cannot be easily defended on moral or realistic grounds."[322] That said, the Qur'an allows people to fight under strict conditions. It states that permission to fight is given for those against whom war has been waged including those who have been evicted from their homes without right or justification (*al-Ḥajj*: 40). Believers who are organized into legitimate and credible political entities are instructed to try their best to make peace between warring parties but if one party is bent on violence then believers must adopt a one-for-all and all-for-one approach in fighting the aggressor until the hostilities end (*al-Ḥujurāt*: 9). When the enemies stop fighting and the persecution has stopped then Muslims must stop as well (*al-Baqarah*: 193). God is with those who restrain themselves (*al-Baqarah*: 194). There should be no fighting with those who are peaceful and who do not partake in aggression.

Any religious text can be used, abused, and manipulated to subjugate and oppress. Religion is not a cure for twisted human mentality and understanding. This is no more evident than in what has come to be identified as the *verse of the sword*, which allowed the Muslim army to kill non-Muslim combatants at a specific historical moment and in a specific context. Most contemporary scholars are perturbed by the fact that traditional jurists site this verse to abrogate "more than two hundred other verses of the Qur'an, all calling for dialogue, freedom of belief, forgiveness, peace and even patience."[323] In fact, God commands believers to be good, generous and merciful toward all peace loving people (*al-Mumtaḥanah*: 8). Many scholars therefore agree that the separation of this allowance to fight from its context is an unacceptable deviation. The verse is clearly situated within the context of war between the pagan Arabs and the Muslim community, where the former were consistently breaking their treaties of peace with the Muslims thereby disturbing commerce, social development, and security.

Even then, an examination of how and when the permission to fight was granted sheds light on its objectives and principles. The Muslims were commanded to make a public declaration that all treaties would be suspended within a four-month period and that during that time the pagans were invited to demonstrate good will and resume full recognition of their alliances (*al-Tawbah*: 2-4). If they desisted from harming the Muslims and life could return to a state of peace and security that was required for collective development and freedom of worship, then there would be no recourse against the pagans. Treaties were not dissolved with those who honored their alliances and did not aid the enemies (*al-Tawbah*: 4). The Qur'an states "so fulfill your engagements with them to the end of their term, for God loves the righteous" (*al-Tawbah*: 4). The objectives of fighting were clear, so that if the enemy conceded hostilities would end immediately (*al-Tawbah*: 5). In other words, peace is the overriding priority. Moreover, those among the pagans who did not wish to fight or be caught in the crossfire were to be protected by the Muslims through temporary asylum and eventually relocation to a place of security (*al-Tawbah*: 6). As for the captives, the Qur'an commands the Prophet as follows: "Oh Prophet, inform the captives who are in your hands that if God finds any good in your hearts, he will give you something better than what has been taken from you, and He will forgive you, for He is Forgiving Merciful" (*al-Anfāl*: 70). This is a most beautiful consolation for prisoners of war and it is a clear indication of how captives are to be treated.

It is clear that Muslims cannot fight indiscriminately. This is a very demanding injunction. The Qur'an calls on believers: "Oh you who believe, if you go out in the cause of God investigate carefully, and do not say to anyone who offers a salutation, 'you are not a believer,' desiring the perishables of the life of this world: with God are endless riches, you were similar [to those in want] once upon a time and God showed you mercy, so clearly investigate and God is aware of what you do" (*al-Nisā'*: 94). This verse encapsulates a very serious war ethic that has long been violated with *advancements* in modern warfare. Fighters cannot kill innocent people and those who make offerings of peace. In short, they are responsible to investigate matters.

Conclusion

Public policy in Islam is primarily an attempt at reform and renewal. The separation of political power and piety in the Divine scheme is intended to encourage the emergence of individuals and groups who are willing to propose and defend what is beneficial while dissuading from what is harmful. It also raises awareness about the necessity of creating institutions that mitigate this reality. Islam is a religion of faith and action. The passing of every era and time requires outstanding individuals and groups who have suitable knowledge and capacity to step up to the challenge of interpreting the Revealed word in relation to contemporaneous conditions. The guidance proffered by this renewal of *Dīn* is intended to help people successfully navigate the challenges of their times. The early history of Islam is very instructive in this regard. The adoption of a new message with its comprehensive social, economic and political reforms led to unprecedented events. This chapter considered seven of that era's timeless lessons and the perspectives that the Muslim community and its leaders had on the integration of the Word with the needs and understanding of their world.

Any reform initiative must have a truthful, clear, logical and useful message. This highlights the principle or objectives orientation of Islamic reform. In addition to respecting fundamental truths, reform is expected to resolve contemporary challenges by integrating appropriate elements from the Revealed and unrevealed word. The knowledge and skills to undertake this challenge demands a certain type of leadership. Leaders must be meritorious, strong and committed but not authoritarian. In fact, they must create the conditions for other qualified leaders in every field of human endeavor to emerge. Individuals and groups whose active engagement is critical for the success of any reform effort. Nevertheless, leadership is only part of the story. We can see from Islam's history that every member of society counts. In particular, the Qur'an gives special attention to the respect and integration of the disabled.

Another important lesson that can be gleaned from Islam's early history is the significance of economics. Reform almost always involves trade-offs and redistribution of resources. Anticipation of losses by individuals and groups leads to strong resistance. While this raises the stakes, it appears to be effective in expediting change. We also learned that throughout comprehensive reform processes, pluralism must be respected and peace prioritized.

NOTES

[1] Professor Jasser Auda is a distinguished professor of Islamic law and its objectives or *maqāṣid*. He is a member of a number of Islamic law academies. Refer to www.jasserauda.net for further information.

[2] *Ṣaḥīḥ al-Bukhārī*, Arabic-English, vol. 8, hadith no. 6094.

[3] Muhammad al-Ghazali, *A Thematic Commentary on the Qur'an* (Malta: IIIT, 2011), p.102.

[4] These include the Mālikīs, Ḥanafīs, Shāfiʿīs, Ḥanbalīs, Jaʿfarīs, Zaydīs, Ẓāhirīs, Ibāḍīs and Muʿtazilīs.

[5] See Ahmad al-Raysuni, *Al-Shura: The Qur'anic Principle of Consultation*, (London: IIIT, 2011), for an engaging exposition of *shūrā* understood as consultation.

[6] Ibn Kathīr, *Al-Bidāyah wa al-Nihāyah* (Dār ʿĀlam al-Kutub, 2003), pp.462-465 includes the debate over the impeachment of Khālid ibn al-Walīd where Abū Bakr clarified a number of his opinions relating to *maqāṣid*. See also Ibn 'Asker, *Tārīkh Damashq* (Beirut: Dār al-Fikr, 1995), vol. 12, p.160, regarding the conversation between Abū Bakr, ʿUmar and Um Ayman regarding the ceasing of Revelation and the need for human ingenuity. Refer also to Aḥmad ibn Ḥajar, *Fatḥ al-Bārī, Sharḥ Ṣaḥīḥ al-Bukhārī* (Cairo: Dār al-Rayyān, 1996), hadith no. 4198, p.759 for Abū Bakr's position on the scope of *shūrā* in conversations over the deployment of Usāmah ibn Zayd as the leader of the Muslim army as Prophet Muhammad had commanded before his death.

[7] Al-Raysuni 2011, p.24.

[8] Jasser Auda, *Maqasid al-Shariah as Philosophy of Islamic Law – A Systems Approach* (London: IIIT, 2008), p.174.

[9] Aziza al-Hibri, *The Islamic Worldview: Islamic Jurisprudence – An Islamic Muslim Perspective* (Chicago: American Bar Association, 2015), p.39.

[10] Mohammad Hashim Kamali, *Freedom of Expression in Islam* (Kuala Lumpur: Ilmiah Publishers, 1998), p.73.

[11] Kamali 1998, p.40.

[12] Ibid.

[13] Ibid.

[14] Al-Raysuni 2011.

[15] Peter M. Haas, "Epistemic Communities and International Policy Coordination", *International*

Organization, 1992, vol. 46, no. 1, p.3.
[16] Ibid.
[17] Ibid., p.4
[18] Ibid., p.28
[19] Auda 2008.
[20] Tariq Ramadan, *Radical Reform – Islamic Ethics and Liberation* (Oxford: Oxford University Press, 2009).
[21] Haas 1992, p.29.
[22] The obligatory nature of *shūrā* is affirmed through its mention alongside three pillars of faith. Arguments that adopting the outcomes of *shūrā* are optional appear to provide a window for authoritarianism and do not conform to the literal word or general spirit of this Qur'anic injunction.
[23] Al-Raysuni 2011, pp.26-40.
[24] Al-Ghazali 2011, p.115.
[25] Muhammad Abdullah Draz, *The Moral World of the Qur'an* (New York: I.B. Tauris, 2008).
[26] Al-Ghazali 2011, p.116.
[27] Ibid., p.252.
[28] Ibid., p.305.
[29] Abū Dawūd, *Sunan Abū Dawūd*, II, 438.
[30] Kamali 1998, p.160, based on Cf A. K. Lambton, *State and Government in Medieval Islam* (Psychology Press, 1981), p.263.
[31] This is a popular narration in the books of biographies (*tarājim*) such as Ibn ᶜAbd al-Barr, Ibn Saᶜd, al-Mazzi, Ibn Ḥajar and Abū Nuᶜaym al-Asbahānī. The narrators of hadith do not narrate this incident except for one narration according to Abū ᶜĀṣim, the authenticity of which is disputed. It is important to recognize, however, that matters of biographies (*tarājim*) are not subject to the sciences of hadith criteria.
[32] Auda 2008, p.10.
[33] Feisal Abdul Rauf, *Defining Islamic Statehood – Measuring and Indexing Contemporary Islamic States* (New York: Palgrave Macmillan, 2015), p.20.
[34] Muhammad al-Tahir Ibn Ashur, *Ibn Ashur Treatise on Maqāṣid al-Shariᶜah* (London: IIIT, 2006), p.98.
[35] Alalwani in Ahmad al-Raysuni, *Imam al-Shatibi's Theory of the Higher Objectives and Intents of Islamic Law* (London: IIIT, 2005), p.xi.
[36] Ibid., p.7.
[37] Abdul Rauf 2015, p.209.
[38] Ibid., p.188; al-Raysuni 2005, p.137.
[39] Al-Alwani in al-Raysuni 2005, p.xiv.
[40] See Draz (2008; chapter 6).
[41] Ibid.
[42] Ibid.
[43] See for instance Qur'an 2:25, 82, 277, 3: 57, 4:57, 122, 173, 5:9, 93, 7:42, 10:4,9, 11:11, 23, 13: 29, 14:23, 18:30, 107, 19:96, 22:14, 23, 50, 56, 24:55, 26:227.
[44] Al-Hibri 2015, p.15.
[45] Abdul Rauf 2015, p.203.
[46] Mahmood in Abdul Rauf 2015, p.174.
[47] Abdul Rauf 2015, p.177.

[48] Auda 2008, p.xxii.
[49]Abdul Rauf 2015, p.175.
[50] *Sunan Abū Dawūd* 2/235.
[51] Al-Asqalānī, *Jawāhir Ṣaḥīḥ al-Bukhārī*, hadith no. 275.
[52] Abdul Rauf 2015, p.202.
[53] Aḥmad 1/194 according to Abdur-Raḥmān ibn Auf, (authentic according to Ahmed Shaker).
[54] Bukhārī.
[55] Bukhārī, hadiths 4341/4342 and 4344/4345, pp.735-756.
[56] Auda 2008, p.xxii.
[57] Kamali in Abdul Rauf 2015, p.18.
[58] Kamali 1998, p.8.
[59] Gamal Eldin Attia, *Towards Realization of the Higher Intents of Islamic Law: Maqāṣid al-Sharīʿah - A Functional Approach* (Washington: IIIT, 2007), p.83.
[60] Al-Raysuni 2005, p.262.
[61] Auda 2008, p.16.
[62] Ibid., p.171.
[63] Attia 2007, p.169.
[64] Muḥammad ibn Jarīr al-Ṭabarī, *Tārīkh al-Umam wa al-Mulūk* (Beirut: Dār al-Kutub al-ʿIlmiyyah, 1407 AH), vol. 3, p.110.
[65] A detailed discussion of the concept of ummah is provided later in this work. For now, it will simply be defined as the imagined community of Muslim believers from all corners of the earth.
[66] Wael Hallaq, *The Impossible State: Islam, Politics and Modernity's Moral Predicament* (New York: Columbia University Press, 2013), Introduction.
[67] Ibid., p.3.
[68] Draz 2008 in reference to the Qur'an 16:93.
[69] Nicholas P. Roberts, *Political Islam and the Invention of Tradition* (Washington: New Academia Publishing), pp.35-74.
[70] Ibid., p.64.
[71] Ebrahim Moosa, "Political Theology in the Aftermath of the Arab Spring," in *The African Renaissance and the Afro-Arab Spring: A Season of Rebirth*, Charles Villa-Vicencio, Erik Doxtader and Ebrahim Moosa (eds.), (Washington: Georgetown University Press, 2015), p.106.
[72] Abū Dawūd, *Sunan Abū Dawūd*, II, p.438.
[73] Ibn Taymiyyah in al-Raysuni 2005, p.35.
[74] M.A. Muqtedar Khan, "Three Dimensions of the Emerging Political Philosophy of Islam," in *Routledge Handbook of Political Islam*, Shahram Akbarzadeh (ed.), (London: Routledge, 2012), p.31.
[75] Al-Raysuni 2005, p.262.
[76] Auda 2008, p.16.
[77] For a detailed presentation of this argument see Taha Jabir Alalwani, *Al-Ummah Magazine,* Issue: 1st Dhu al-Hijjah, 1430 AH.
[78] Kamali 1998, p.45.
[79] Ibid., p.46.
[80] Moosa 2015, p.112.
[81] Anne-Sophie Roald, *Women in Islam – The Western Experience* (London: Routledge, 2001), p.10.
[82] Attia 2007, p.85.
[83] Al-Hibri 2015, p.40.

[84] Auda 2008, p.61.
[85] Ramadan 2009, p.131.
[86] See for instance Mohammad Akram Nadwi, *Al-Muḥaddithāt: The Women Scholars in Islam*, 2nd revised edition, (Interface Publications Ltd., 2013). As well as, Omar Reda Kahala, *Aʿlām al-Nisā' fī ʿAlamay al-ʿArab wa al-Islām*, 5th edition, (Beirut: Al-Risālah, 1985).
[87] Abdul Rauf 2015, p.33.
[88] According to Blichner and Molander, juridification has a number of dimensions including "constitutive juridification, juridification as law's expansion and differentiation, as increased conflict solving with reference to law, as increased judicial power and as legal framing." Lars Blichner and Anders Molander, "What is Juridification?" Centre for European Studies, University of Oslo, Working Paper no. 14, March 2005, p.1.
[89] Al-Raysuni 2005, p.xv.
[90] Moosa 2015, p.117.
[91] Ibid.
[92] Al-Ghazali 2011, p.103.
[93] In al-Raysuni 2005, p.xi.
[94] See Auda 2008, pp.20-21 and al-Raysuni 2005.
[95] Al-Raysuni 2005, p.xxxvi.
[96] Al-Shāṭibī, *Al-Muwāfaqāt*, vol. 2, p.25.
[97] Ibn Qayyim al-Jawziyyah, *Iʿlām al-Muwaqqiʿīn ʿan Rabb al-ʿAlamīn,* (Beirut: Dār al-Fikr, n.d.), 3/11.
[98] Al-Raysuni 2005, p.13.
[99] Auda 2008, p.61.
[100] Abul-Qasim ibn Abd al-Hakam, *Futūḥ Maṣr* (Leiden: Brill, 1920), p.290.
[101] See for instance, Syed Ameer Ali, *Short History of the Saracens* (Suffolk: Richard Clay and Company, Ltd., 1927) and Will Durant, *The Story of Civilization* (New York: Simon & Schuster, 1950) on the administrative innovations of Arab rule.
[102] See Auda (2015) for his discussion of Ibn Khaldūn's ideas on the downfall of the office of the caliph. Jasser Auda, *Al-Dawlah al-Madaniyyah* (Beirut: Al-Shabakah al-ʿArabiyyah, 2015), p.21.
[103] Hallaq 2013, p.29.
[104] Ibid., p.52.
[105] Even before Hallaq's work which argued that this period was characterized by a Shariʿah *paradigm*, Yusuf al-Qaradawi had elaborated that the Shariʿah was the predominant paradigm during Islam's dynastic phase. In his study perceptions of government failure are written off as human failure. Yusuf al-Qaradawi, *Tārīkhunā al-Muftarā ʿAlayhi* (Cairo: Al-Shurūq, 2006). In doing so, neither scholar presents a convincing account of why the Islamic world not only eventually came under foreign control but to date has been incapable of ridding itself of tyranny and corruption.
[106] Attia 2007, p.35.
[107] S.M. Ghazanfar and Azim Islahi, "Explorations in Medieval Arab-Islamic Economic Thought: Some

Aspects of Ibn Taimiyah's Economics," in *Medieval Islamic Economic Thought – Fillling the "Great Gap" in European Economics*, Ghazanfar, S.M. (ed.), (London: Routledge Curzon, 2003), p.56.

[108] Hallaq 2013, p.67.

[109] Ibid.

[110] Ameer Ali Syed, *A Short History of the Saracens* (UK: 1927), p.72.

[111] Ibid.

[112] Ibid., p.77.

[113] Auda 2008, p.4.

[114] Kamali in Abdul Rauf 2015, p.217.

[115] Auda 2008, p.19.

[116] Attia 2007, p.79.

[117] Abdul Rauf 2015, p.27.

[118] Auda 2008, p.22.

[119] Attia 2007, p.1.

[120] Ibid., p.1.

[121] For a detailed elaboration on each refer to Auda 2008, chapter 4.

[122] Al-Raysuni 2005, p.281

[123] Ibid.

[124] Auda 2008, p.21

[125] Ibid.

[126] The scholars include Ahmad Abbadi, Jasser Auda, Osman Bakar, Anies Baswedan, the late Mahmood Ahmed Ghazi, Khanjar Hamieh, Mohammad Hashim Kamali, Mohammad Javad Larijani, Ahmad Syafii Maarif, Tahir Mahmood, Abdul Hamid Mohamad, and Recep Senturk. For brief bios of each scholar refer to Abdul Rauf 2015, pp.xiii-xv.

[127] Abdul Rauf 2015, p.63.

[128] Senturk in Abdul Rauf 2015, p.65.

[129] Auda 2008, p.24.

[130] Al-Ghazali 2011, p.14.

[131] Al-Ghazali in al-Raysuni 2005, p.19.

[132] Abdul Rauf 2015, p.67.

[133] The first stage in embryonic development occurs when the fertilized egg (blastocyst) clings or adheres to the uterine lining of the mother. In essence it is the act by which the embryo clings to life, to survival. For in that process of implantation the embryo absorbs oxygen and nutrition from the uterine lining without which no pregnancy occurs and no individual results. In other words, if not for our inherent need to adhere and our associated dependence on the environment within the womb we would not come to be.

[134] Auda 2008. p.22.

[135] Abdul Rauf 2015. pp.70-72.

[136] Ibid., p.72.

[137] Ramadan 2009. p.127.

[138] Ibid., p.131.

[139] Qur'an 12:2, 13: 37, 16:103, 39:28, etc.

[140] In an authentic Prophetic narration, ʿĀ'ishah tells us that the Prophet exhorted Abū Bakr to be tolerant when he scolded ʿĀ'ishah for allowing singing and musical instruments near the Prophet. The Prophet's response was: "Leave them alone." We are also told that on one occasion during Eid when a group of Abyssinians were playing with

shields and spears, the Prophet stood with ʿĀ'ishah behind him so that their cheeks were touching as they watched the performers play and dance. The Prophet even encouraged them to continue, saying: "Carry on, O tribe of Arfida." They stood watching until ʿĀ'ishah got tired. *Ṣaḥīḥ al-Bukhārī 907, Ṣaḥīḥ Muslim* 892.

[141] Ibn Ashur 2006, p.247.
[142] Auda 2008, p.22.
[143] Abdul Rauf 2015, p.69.
[144] Auda 2008, p.24.
[145] Abdul Rauf 2015, p.72.
[146] Gauhar in Abdul Rauf 2015, p.73.
[147] Ibid.
[148] Auda 2008, p.10.
[149] *Sunan Ibn Mājah*, 2473 in Abdul Rauf 2015, p.74.
[150] Auda 2008, p.23.
[151] Abdul Rauf 2015, p.75.
[152] Ibid.
[153] Abdul Rauf 2015, p.75.
[154] Ibid., p.209.
[155] Attia 2007, p.12.
[156] Ṭabarānī, 901 – Hathami, 98/4 – al-Suyouṭi, 5232.
[157] Ibn Ashur 2006, p.169.
[158] Auda 2008, p.xxii.
[159] Abdul Rauf 2015, p.17.
[160] Auda 2008, p.199.
[161] Ibid., p.56.
[162] Ibid., p.xxii.
[163] Ibid., p.187.
[164] Attia 2007, p.68.
[165] Ibid.; Abdul Rauf 2015.
[166] Auda 2008, p.221.
[167] Ibid.
[168] Ibid., p.220.
[169] Al-Raysuni 2015, p.278.
[170] *Sunan Daraqutni*, 'Ashribah', hadith 104, vol. 2/4, p.289.
[171] Al-Hibri 2015, p.67.
[172] Al-Raysuni 2005, p.262.
[173] Ramadan 2009, p.4.
[174] Ibid.
[175] Ibid., p.21.
[176] Ibid., p.92.
[177] Ibid., p.85.
[178] Ibid., p.92.
[179] Taha Jabir Alalwani, *Towards a Fiqh for Minorities – Some Basic Reflections*, New Revised Edition, Occasional Paper Series 18, (London: IIIT, 2003), pp.14-15.
[180] Ibid., p.116.
[181] Ibid.
[182] Ibid., p.109.
[183] Ibid., p.128.
[184] Alalwani 2003, p.15.
[185] Ramadan 2009, p.4.
[186] Ibid., p.130.
[187] Ibid., p.131.
[188] Ibid., p.117 and then pp.242-244.
[189] Ibid., p.89.
[190] Alalwani 2003, p.16.
[191] Auda 2008, p.253.
[192] Ibid., p.xxvi.
[193] Ibid., p.142.
[194] Ibid., p.191.
[195] Ibid., p.195.
[196] Ibid., p.198.
[197] Ibid., p.206.
[198] Ibid., p.228.
[199] Ibid., p.232.
[200] Adapted from Draz 2008, p.8.
[201] See chapter 1 for further details on the SIP.

[202] Kamali 2015, p.11.
[203] Ibid., p.12.
[204] Ibid., p.13.
[205] Yusuf al-Qaradawi, *Al-Siyāsah al-Sharʿiyyah fi Ḍaw' Nuṣūṣ al-Sharīʿah wa Maqsiduhā*, 2nd edn., (Cairo: Maktabah Wahbah, 2005).
[206] Ibid., p.313.
[207] Auda 2008, p.23.
[208] see for instance Jasser Auda in Abdul Rauf 2015, p.242.
[209] Renowned Islamic scholars like Mohammed Selim al-Awwa, Yusuf al-Qaradawi, Allal al-Fasi, al-Tahir ibn Ashur, Gamal Eldin Attia, Hassan al-Turabi, and Rachid Ghannoushi among others have addressed this subject in various ways.
[210] *Al-Bidāyah wa al-Nihāyah*, vol. 6, pp.305-306.
[211] Kamali 1998, p.21.
[212] Ibid., p.2.
[213] Senturk in Abdul Rauf 2015, p.25.
[214] Abdul Rauf 2015, p.21.
[215] Kamali 1998, p.27.
[216] Ibid.
[217] Abdul Raouf 2015, p.22.
[218] Jāmiʿ al-Tirmidhī 41:2687.
[219] *Nahjul Balaghah*, saying 79. http://dawoodi-bohras.com/pdfs/Nahjul-Balagah-English.pdf accessed March 4, 2016
[220] Auda 2008, p.23.
[221] See Eva Brems, *Human Rights: Universality and Diversity* (London: Martinus Nijhoff Publishers, 2001) for an excellent and comprehensive legal critique.
[222] Auda 2008, p.1.
[223] Ibid., p.24.
[224] Abdul Rauf 2015, p.63.
[225] Auda 2008, p.23.
[226] Abdul Rauf 2015, p.75.
[227] Ibid., p.75.
[228] Kamali 1998, p.8.
[229] Subhi Mahmassani, *Arkān Huqūq al-Insān fī al-Islām* (Beirut: Dar al-ʿIlm li al-Malayin, 1979), p.72, cited in Kamali 1998, p.7.
[230] David H. Bailey, *Public Liberties*, (Chicago: Rand, McNally, 1964), p.27 cited in Kamali 1998, p.24.
[231] Kamali 1998, p.166.
[232] Ibid., p.241.
[233] Ibid., p.24.
[234] Ibid., p.189.
[235] Ibid., p.30
[236] Ibid., p.31.
[237] Ibid., p.30.
[238] Ibid., p.31.
[239] Attia 2007, p.83.
[240] Ibid.
[241] Ismail al-Hasani, *Naẓariyyah al-Maqāṣid ʿInd al-Imām Muḥammad al-Ṭāhir ibn ʿAshūr* (London: IIIT, 1995), p.299.
[242] Narrated by al-Marwazi in *Taʿẓīm Qadr al-Ṣalāh*, according to Abū al-ʿAlā' ibn al-Shikhīr.
[243] Narrated by al-Dārquṭnī in *Al-Mustajad*, and al-Kharā'iṭ in *Makārim al-Akhlāq*, both according to Abū Sa'īd al-Khudrī.
[244] Abdul Rauf 2015, p.27.
[245] Ibid., p.34.
[246] Qur'an 2:229, 230; 65:1.
[247] Draz 2008, p.105.
[248] Merriam-Webster Online.

http://www.merriam-webster.com/dictionary/dignity accessed April 15, 2016.
[249] Senturk in Abdul Rauf 2015, p.23
[250] Ibn Ashur 2006, p.47.
[251] Qur'an 19:84, 46:35, 16:1.
[252] Muslim on the authority of Abū Hurayrah.
[253] *Fiqh-us-Sunnah*, vol. 3, p.98.
[254] Draz 2008, p.5.
[255] Ibid., p.287.
[256] Ibid.
[257] Muslim on the authority of Abū Sa'īd al-Khudrī.
[258] Andrew Fagan, "Human Rights," *The Internet Encyclopedia of Philosophy*, ISSN 2161-0002, http://www.iep.utm.edu/, accessed April 12, 2016.
[259] Draz 2008, p.289.
[260] Muslim in the authority of Abū Hurayrah.
[261] Draz 2008, p.289.
[262] Ibid.
[263] Bukhārī and Muslim on the authority of Anas.
[264] Draz 2008.
[265] Ibid., p.18.
[266] Ibid., p.70.
[267] Ibid., p.288.
[268] Related by Abū Dāwūd (4291) and was verified as *Ṣaḥīḥ* by al-Sakhāwy in *al-Maqāṣid al-Ḥasanah* (149) and al-Albāny in *al-Silsilah al-Ṣaḥīḥah* (599).
[269] Abdul Rauf 2015, p.33.
[270] Ismāʿīl Rājī al Fārūqī, *Al Tawḥīd: Its Implications for Thought and Life* (Herndon: IIIT, 1992), p.10.
[271] Ibid.
[272] Ibid., p.11.
[273] Draz 2008, p.65.
[274] Al-Faruqi 1992, p.10.
[275] Ibid., p.11.
[276] Qur'an 32:7; 87:2; 40:64.
[277] Al-Faruqi 1992, p.12.
[278] Draz 2008.
[279] Al-Raysuni 2005, Attia 2007.
[280] Attia 2007, p.97.
[281] Al-Raysuni 2005, p.32.
[282] Abdul Rauf 2015, p.50.
[283] Kamali 2015, p.3.
[284] Ibn Ashur 2006, pp.99-100.
[285] Ibid., p.100.
[286] Ibid., p.117.
[287] Ibid., p.97.
[288] Ibid.
[289] Al-Qaradawi 2005, p.307 and discussed in Kamali 2015, p.15.
[290] Al-Qaradawi 2005, pp.301-302.
[291] Kamali 2015, p.15.
[292] Qur'an 3: 113; 5:66; 7:159; 32:24.
[293] Qur'an 1:126; 7:57, 58; 14:35; 16:7; 25:49; 27:91; 34:15; 35:9; 43: 11; 50:11; 90:1,2; 95:3; 3: 1; 40:4; 50:36; 89:8,11.
[294] Abul Faraj ibn al-Jawzī, *Manāqib Amīr al-Mu'minīn ʿUmar ibn al-Khaṭṭāb* (Dubai: Dār Ibn Khaldūn, 1996).
[295] See for instance Abū al-Fidā' Ismāʿīl ibn Kathīr, *Tafsīr al-Qur'an al-ʿAẓām* (Dār Ṭībah, 2002), p.216 and Muhammad Rashid Rida, *Tafsīr al-Manār li Muḥammad ʿAbdū* (Al-Hay'ah al-Miṣriyyah li al-Kitāb), p.210.

[296] Merriam-Webster Online. http://www.merriam-webster.com/dictionary/dignity accessed April 15, 2016.
[297] Qur'an 59:1; 61:1; 62:1; 64:1.
[298] Bukhārī and Muslim.
[299] Muslim on the authority of Jābir and Ibn ᶜAbbās.
[300] Bukhārī on the authority of Abū Hurayrah, hadith no. 2856; Muslim on the authority of Abū Hurayrah, *Bāb al-nahy ᶜan qatl al-naml* (the forbidding of killing ants), hadith no. 2241 and in other collections.
[301] Bukhārī and Muslim.
[302] Related by Abū Dāwūd (4291) and was verified as *Ṣaḥīḥ* by al-Sakhāwy in *al-Maqāṣid al-Ḥasanah* (149) and al-Albāny in *al-Silsilah al-Ṣaḥīḥah* (599).
[303] Al-Ghazali 2011, p.3.
[304] Qur'an 2:179; 6:122; 8:24; 16:97
[305] Reflect on the spiritual power of the mother of Mary, the mother of Moses, Mary mother of Jesus, the wife of Pharaoh Asseya, and other women to whom God had responded to directly in the Qur'an. There are also many recognized examples in the Sunnah including Khadījah, first wife of the Prophet, and Faṭimah his daughter, and other female Companions (early Muslim converts).
[306] Al-Raysuni 2011, pp.78-79.
[307] Al-Ghazali 2011, p.40.
[308] Draz 2008, p.285.
[309] Attia 2007, p.73.
[310] Al-Tirmidhī, Sunan, '*Kitāb Ṣifāt al-Qiyāmah,*' Bāb 1.
[311] Refer to Draz (2008) pp.363-364 endnotes 112-162 for a full list of the verses supporting these statements.
[312] Refer to Draz (2008) p.365 endnotes 207-245 for a full list of the verses supporting these statements.
[313] Bukhārī 1623, 1626, 6361; Muslim 98; al-Tirmidhī 1628, 2046, 2085; Ibn Ḥanbal, *Musnad* 19774.
[314] *Al-Bidāyah wa al-Nihāyah* 6:305-306.
[315] http://www.alim.org/library/biography/khalifa/content/KUM/13/pdf/2After accessed February 15, 2018.
[316] *Musnad* Imām Aḥmad, 6/118.
[317] See endnote 31.
[318] Al-Ghazali 2011, p.28.
[319] Qur'an 3:130; 4:161; 30:39; 2:275.
[320] Muhammad Abdullah Draz, *Al-Ribā fī Naẓar al-Qānūn al-Islāmī* (Al-ᶜAṣr al-Ḥadīth lī al-Nashr, 1987).
[321] Ibn Kathīr 1998; vol.II; p.212.
[322] Al-Ghazali 2011, p.18.
[323] Auda 2008, p.222.

BIBLIOGRAPHY

Abdul Karim Sorouch,"Tolerance and Governance: A Discourse on Religion and Democracy", in *Reason, Freedom and Democracy in Islam: Essential Writings of Abdul Karim Soroush*, M. Sadri and S. Sadri (trans. and ed.), (New York: Oxford University Press, 2000).

Abdulaziz Sachedina, *The Islamic Roots of Democratic Pluralism* (New York: Oxford University Press, 2001).

——, "The Role of Islam in the Public Square: Guidance or Governance?" ISIM Paper No. 5 (Amsterdam: Amsterdam University Press, 2006).

Abū al-Fidā' Ismāʿīl ibn Kathīr, *The Life of the Prophet Muhammad – Al-Sira al-Nabawiyya*, volumes I-IV, Mustafa Abd al-Wahid (ed.), trans. Dr. Trevor le Gassick, The Centre for Muslim Contribution to Civilization, (Reading: Garnet Publishing, 1998).

——, *Tafsīr al-Qur'an al-ʿAẓām* (Dār Ṭībah, 2002).

Abul Faraj ibn al-Jawzī, *Manāqib Amīr al-Mu'minīn ʿUmar ibn al-Khaṭṭāb* (Dubai: Dār Ibn Khaldūn, 1996).

Ahmad al-Raysuni, *Imam al-Shatibi's Theory of the Higher Objectives and Intents of Islamic Law* (London: IIIT, 2005).

——, *Al-Shura: The Qur'anic Principle of Consultation* (London: IIIT, 2011).

Ahmed S. Moussalli, "Sayyid Qutb – Founder of Radical Political Islamic Ideology," in *Routledge Handbook of Political Islam*, Shahram Akbarzadeh (ed.), (London: Routledge, 2012), pp.9-26.

Amartya Sen, "Elements of a Theory of Human Rights," *Philosophy and Public Affairs*, 2004, vol. 32, no. 4.

Ameer Ali Syed, *A Short History of the Saracens* (UK: 1927).

Andrew Fagan, "Human Rights," *The Internet Encyclopedia of Philosophy*, ISSN 2161-0002, http://www.iep.utm.edu/, accessed April 12, 2016.

Anne-Sophie Roald, *Women in Islam – The Western Experience* (London: Routledge, 2001).

Aziza al-Hibri, *The Islamic Worldview: Islamic Jurisprudence – An Islamic Muslim Perspective* (Chicago: American Bar Association, 2015).

Ebrahim Moosa, "Political Theology in the Aftermath of the Arab Spring," in *The African Renaissance and the Afro-Arab Spring: A Season of Rebirth*, Charles Villa-Vicencio, Erik Doxtader and Ebrahim Moosa (eds.), (Washington: Georgetown University Press, 2015).

Eva Brems, *Human Rights: Universality and Diversity* (London: Martinus Nijhoff Publishers, 2001).

Feisal Abdul Rauf, *Defining Islamic Statehood – Measuring and Indexing Contemporary Islamic States* (New York: Palgrave Macmillan, 2015).

Gamal Eldin Attia, *Towards Realization of the Higher Intents of Islamic Law: Maqāṣid Al Shari'ah A Functional Approach* (Washington: IIIT, 2007).

Internet Encyclopedia of Philosophy http://www.iep.utm.edu/hum-rts/ accessed April 8, 2016.

Ismail al-Hasani, *Naẓariyyah al-Maqāṣid ʿInd al-Imām Muḥammad al-Ṭāhir ibn ʿAshūr* (London: IIIT, 1995).

Ismāʿīl Rājī al Fārūqī, *Al Tawḥīd: Its Implications for Thought and Life* (Herndon: IIIT, 1992).

Jasser Auda, *Al-Dawlah al-Madaniyyah* (Beirut: Al-Shabakah al-ʿArabiyyah, 2015).

——, *Fiqh al-Maqāṣid: Ināṭāt al-Aḥkām al-Sharʿiyyah bi Maqāṣidiha,* 3rd edn., (Herndon: IIIT 2008a).

——, *Maqasid al-Shariah as Philosophy of Islamic Law – A Systems Approach* (London: IIIT, 2008).

John Esposito and John Voll, "Islam and the West: Muslim Voices in Dialogue," *Millennium Journal of International Studies*, 2000, vol. 29, no. 3, pp.613-39.

Lars Blichner and Anders Molander, "What is Juridification?" Centre for European Studies, University of Oslo, Working Paper No. 14, March 2005.

M.A. Muqtedar Khan, "Three Dimensions of the Emerging Political Philosophy of Islam," in *Routledge Handbook of Political Islam*, Shahram Akbarzadeh (ed.), (London: Routledge, 2012), pp.27-34.

Mohammad Hashim Kamali, *Freedom of Expression in Islam* (Kuala Lumpur: Ilmiah Publishers, 1998).

Mohammed Ayoob, "Political Islam: Image and Reality," *World Policy Journal*, 2004, vol. 21, no. 3, pp.1-14.

Muhammad Abdullah Draz, *Al-Ribā fī Naẓar al-Qānūn al-Islāmī* (Al-ʿAṣr al-Ḥadīth lī al-Nashr, 1987).

——, *The Moral World of the Qur'an* (New York: I.B. Tauris, 2008).

Muhammed al-Ghazali, *A Thematic Commentary on the Qur'an* (Malta: IIIT, 2011).

Muhammad al-Tahir Ibn Ashur, *Ibn Ashur: Treatise on Maqāṣid al-Shariʿah* (London: IIIT, 2006).

Muḥammad ibn Jarīr al-Ṭabarī, *Tārīkh al-Umam wa al-Mulūk* (Beirut: Dār al-Kutub al-ʿIlmiyyah, 1407 AH).

Muhammad Rashid Rida, *Tafsīr al-Manār li Muḥammad ʿAbdū* (Al-Hay'ah al-Miṣriyyah li al-Kitāb, n.d.).

Nicholas P. Roberts, *Political Islam and the Invention of Tradition* (Washington: New Academia Publishing, 2015).

Peter M. Haas, "Epistemic Communities and International Policy Coordination", *International Organization*, 1992, vol. 46, no. 1, pp.1-35.

S.M. Ghazanfar and Azim Islahi, "Explorations in Medieval Arab-Islamic Economic Thought: Some Aspects of Ibn Taimiyah's Economics," in *Medieval Islamic Economic Thought – Fillling the "Great Gap" in European Economics*, Ghazanfar, S.M. (ed.), (London: Routledge Curzon, 2003), pp.53-71.

Safi-ur-Rahman al-Mubarakpuri, *Al-Rahīq al-Makhtūm (The Sealed Nectar) – Biography of the Noble Prophet* (Riyadh: Maktabah Dār al-Salām, 1995).

Shahram Akbarzadeh, "The Paradox of Political Islam," in *Routledge Handbook of Political Islam*, Shahram Akbarzadeh (ed.), (New York: Routledge, 2012), pp 1-8.

Taha Jabir Alalwani, *Towards a Fiqh For Minorities – Some Basic Reflections*, New Revised Edition, Occasional Paper Series 18, (London: IIIT, 2003).

Tariq Ramadan, *Radical Reform – Islamic Ethics and Liberation* (Oxford: Oxford University Press, 2009).

——, "The Role of Islam in the Public Square: Guidance or Governance?", in *Islamic Democratic Discourse: Theory, Debates, and Philosophical Perspectives*, M.A. Muqtedar Khan (ed.), (New York: Lexington Books, 2006).

Thomas D. Seeley, *Honeybee Democracy* (Princeton: Princeton University Press, 2010).

Wael Hallaq, *The Impossible State: Islam, Politics and Modernity's Moral Predicament* (New York: Columbia University Press, 2013).

Will Durant, *The Age of Faith: A History of Medieval Civilization – Christian, Islamic, and Judaic – From Constantine to Dante: A.D. 325-1300* (New York: Simon and Schuster, 1950).

William Sweet, "Jeremy Bentham (1748-1832)," *The Internet Encyclopedia of Philosophy*, ISSN 2161-0002, http://www.iep.utm.edu/, accessed April 12, 2016.

Yahya Muhammad, "Naẓariyyah al-Maqāṣid wa al-Wāqiʿ", *Qaḍāyā Islāmiyyah Muʿāṣirah*, 8, p.150.

Yusuf al-Qaradawi, *Al-Siyāsah al-Sharʿiyyah fi Ḍaw' Nuṣūṣ al-Sharīʿah wa Maqsiduhā*, 2nd edn, (Cairo: Maktabah Wahbah, 2005).

——, *Tarīkhunā al-Muftarā ʿAlayhi* (Cairo: Dār al-Shurūq, 2006).